SCAM school

Your Guide to Scoring Free Drinks,

Doing Magic &

Becoming the Life of the Party

by Brian Brushwood

Illustrations by
Jon Tilton and Brandt Hughes

SKYHORSE PUBLISHING

Skyhorse Publishing books may be purchased in bulk at special discounts for sales promotion, corporate gifts, fund-raising, or educational purposes. Special editions can also be created to specifications. For details, contact the Special Sales Department, Skyhorse Publishing, 307 West 36th Street, 11th Floor, New York, NY 10018 or info@skyhorsepublishing.com.

Skyhorse® and Skyhorse Publishing® are registered trade-marks of Skyhorse Publishing, Inc.®, a Delaware corporation.

Visit our website at www.skyhorsepublishing.com.

10 9 8 7 6 5 4 3 2

Library of Congress Cataloging-in-Publication Data
Brushwood, Brian.
  Scam school : your guide to scoring free drinks, doing magic, and becoming the life of the party / Brian Brushwood.
     pages cm
  ISBN 978-1-62087-854-5 (pbk. : alk. paper) 1. Magic tricks. 2. Telepathy. 3. Fraud. I. Title.
  GV1547.B88 2013
  793.8--dc23
                                                2013002595

Printed in the United States of America

This book is dedicated to the extraordinarily talented magicians who have lent their routines, ideas, encouragement and expertise to Scam School over the last five years. There simply isn't room to include them all, but I want to give special thanks to Michael Ammar, Banachek, Pete Boie, Steve Daly, Eric Dittelman, Rich Ferguson, Danny Garcia, Martin Gardner, Dr. James Grime, Daniel Martin, Andrew Mayne, Robert Neale, Todd Robbins, Mike Powers, MIT Rob, Robert Strong, Diamond Jim Tyler, and Jonny Zavant for personally helping to make Scam School the very best show it can be.

contents

CONTENTS

introduction

Four years and over 200 episodes ago, I pitched Scam School to Revision3 as "the only show dedicated to social engineering at the bar on the street." I wanted to cover everything from street crime, cons, and hustles to bar scams, mind-reading, and magic tricks . . . and not just from an academic standpoint. I wanted to get out there, in the actual bars, and teach these effects to real people.

What came out of that pitch has been one of the most exciting, terrifying, and transformative experiences of my life. I've received thousands of emails from all over the world thanking me for the show . . . and hundreds of YouTube comments telling me to shave off my ridiculous hair. From the middle-school kid in Bulgaria thanking me for making him popular at school, to the close online friendships I've made through the show, I'm endlessly thankful, both for the connections Scam School has made possible and for the growth it's brought me as a performer.

People have been asking me for years to create a singular resource for all of the scams and tricks covered on Scam School. Before now, it would take you almost 50 hours just to watch every episode of Scam School (. . . and you'd have to take your own notes).

Thanks to the magic of media ehanced books, we are able to create a super-dense resource, packed with audio commentary, video illustrations, and detailed instructions for over 80 effects.

You'll notice each effect is given its own category: opener, tweener, or closer. We've mentioned this in a couple of Scam School episodes, but here's what they mean:

Openers: Effects that require no attention or effort from your target audience. Bars and parties are inherently chaotic environments, and your first effect should be one that will always work, whether someone's paying attention or not. These effects should cause people to stop and shout "Do that again!" (Hint: never repeat a trick. Once is a trick, twice is a lesson. Instead, move on to . . .)

Tweeners: Effects that require participation or extended focus from your targets. Maybe they need to remember a card, or maybe there's just enough process in the trick that you only want to perform it for people who want to see magic. These effects usually have more powerful impacts and help to build momentum with your audience.

Closers: Effects where you translate your momentum into getting a free drink, the girl's phone number, or anything else you want. These are unbeatable challenges that offer you an opportunity to ask for something in exchange for an answer. They re-establish you as the person in charge of the social interaction, and you can use them to cement a precedent of "pay-for-play": You're happy to keep entertaining the crowd, as long as those free drinks keep coming.

(If you want to hear more about these, check out my TEDx talk, "How to Scam Your Way into Anything.")

about brian

Since 2000, Brian Brushwood has been touring nationally and internationally with his "Bizarre Magic" show . . . a thrill-ride mashup of dangerous stunts, fire-eating, mind-reading and comedy magic. He's appeared twice on "The Tonight Show with Jay Leno," as well as dozens of national TV programs nationwide. He's headlined three times at Universal Orlando's "Halloween Horror Nights," performing live on-stage for over 200,000 people, and just last year was seen by over 70 million people on 2 live Indonesian TV magic specials.

In 2004, Brian began his first touring stage lecture, "Scams, Sasquatch, and the Supernatural: an Amazing Exposure of Pseudoscience." College audiences nationwide learn the tricks and techniques used by fake psychics, astrologers, and people who claim to speak with the dead.

Later, Brian started giving his talk "Social Engineering: Scam Your Way into Anything," an exploration of the psychology of scammers and con artists. In this talk, Brian teaches his audience how to use simple psychological tricks to achieve anything from talking their way out of a ticket to

= independently (

sneaking backstage at concerts . . . and, most importantly, how to recognize when someone's trying to manipulate them.

In 2008, Brian began hosting Scam School, the "only show dedicated to social engineering at the bar and on the street." Viewers learn quick 5-minute tips and tricks to score free drinks or to scam their friends. The show was named a "Top Video Podcast" of 2008 and 2009 by iTunes, and as of 2013, Scam School sports a back catalog of almost 300 episodes, racking up over 2 million views per month.

In 2009, Brian launched NSFW with co-host Justin Robert Young. The show is raw, outrageous and totally live. On November 1, 2011, NSFW celebrated its 100th episode, and continues to broadcast live shows every Tuesday night. A variety of celebrity guests have been featured on NSFW, including Greg Grunberg,

Michael Rooker, and Romany Malco. NSFW's rabid fan base known as "chatrealm" documents the show's crazy adventures on

the BBpedia (at bbpedia.net), a comprehensive online collection of all things Brian Brushwood. iTunes named NSFW a "Top Audio Podcast" of 2010.

Since then, Brian has hosted and co-hosted several other shows, including Frame Rate with Tom Merritt, the Weird Things Podcast, Game On! with Veronica Belmont, and more.

In addition to this book, Brian has also authored *The Professional's Guide to Fire Eating*, *Pack the House*, and *Cheats Cons Swindles and Tricks: 57 Ways to Scam a Free Drink*.

Visit shwood.com for information about his books, tour schedule, or to book an event.

17 years ago: the day Teller gave me
the secret to my career in magic.

Lately a lot of young magicians have been asking me for advice, which has caused me to remember one of the most valuable correspondences of my life: one of the most mind-blowing letters I ever received, chock-full of insights that to this very day guide my career and philosophy in both creating and performing magic.

This is a pretty long chapter, but with Teller's permission, I'd like to share with you *the secrets he gave me 17 years ago to starting a successful career in magic.*

First, a bit of back-story: Penn and Teller have been my heroes in magic since I was 8 years old. Back when I would watch just about anything related to magic, P&T were special because they were so damned cool. They'd connect with their audience, let them on the inside . . . even teach them some tricks to do at home. I was hooked.

By the time I was 19, I was a decent semi-professional magician, trying desperately to figure out both who I wanted to be onstage and what I had to say. Then, during the summer of 1994, I got my first

chance to see Penn and
Teller live. I drove three and a
half hours with my best
friend Gordon to watch the
performance and (more
importantly) get the chance to
meet them afterwards.

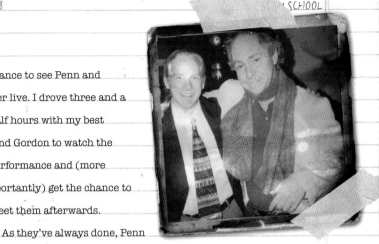

    As they've always done, Penn
and Teller hung out in the lobby after the show to meet
anyone who'd like to say hello. While we waited in line, Gordon
and I started brainstorming ways to stand out from the crowd and
how to make an impression on my heroes. Gordon had a hilarious idea
that he was too chicken to try, so with his permission, I asked
Teller to sign my three of clubs ". . . to my bastard son, Brian."

    I was totally jazzed when this got a laugh from Teller, and
positively giddy to spend the next few minutes talking to one of my
heroes about how to get started in magic . . . Best. Show. Ever.

    One year later, I was much more serious about magic, and much
more frustrated as I was still struggling to find my own voice,
character, and presentation. That's when I happened upon Teller's
email address, and in a fit of frustration-induced bravery, wrote
the following letter:

Date: **Tuesday, Oct 17, 1995**
From: **"Brian Allen Brushwood"**
Subject: **Fury**
To: **"Teller"**

All right. I have put it off long enough. I told myself I would wait to write you until I had something meaningful to say, but I have been sitting on your address (figuratively) for months now, and am fed up with waiting.

The fact is, Teller, I am furious at you.

Not for offending anyone, for being outrageous, or for being so inventive with your magic, but because you were there first. In Genii magazine, you make a brilliant point of explaining that regardless of the true origin of a trick, whoever is most famous performing it OWNS it (I believe you cited your new "ownership" the bullet catch). Unfortunately, I don't believe you extended this idea far enough. This concept reaches all the way into the very attitudes and styles of performance. In short, because of Penn and Teller, I cannot be angry at magic, at least not on stage.

It seems to me, that just as you own the Bullet Catch, so do you own the ability to lash out at magic, to act as a vent for your audiences frustrations with the cruise-ship trickymen. Not to mention the use of blood and/or violence in a humorous way. Hell! You might even own the two-male duo! All this ownership has kept me from doing the kind of stage (and close-up, believe it or not) magic I want, for fear of being branded a copycat.

This summer, I attempted to tackle this problem by writing a couple of two male duo acts, trying my damnedest to keep the P&T out of my veins; it met with some success. One act, consisting of two comedy magic character pieces (A drill instructor who performs the "coloring book". A gibberish-speaking samurai who performs a card-trick that ends in Hara-kiri) won the Texas Association of Magicians Senior Comedy competition. However, I find it difficult to follow your advice of "letting hate, not love, be your driving force" (which is absolutely true) and at the same time keep from becoming a P&T wannabe.

If you could offer any advice on how you established your own character and style, I would greatly appreciate it.

Brian Allen Brushwood

Just writing the letter was cathartic . . . I mean after all, who was I to Teller? I would have been perfectly happy to get a five word courtesy response, but to my absolute astonishment, the next morning I found the following mind-blowing essay in my inbox:

From: "Teller"

Subject: Fury

To: "Brian Allen Brushwood"

My dear bastard son,

It is about time you wrote, my boy.

Now, calm down. Remind yourself of a few things.

I am 47. I have been earning my living in show business for twenty years. I have been doing magic since I was five, which makes it 42 years. And I had the good fortune to (a) meet Penn and (b) become an off-Broadway hit at the exact right moment in time.

When we started we HAD no style, no understanding of ourselves or what we were doing. We had feelings, vague ones, a sense of what we liked, maybe, but no unified point of view, not even a real way to express our partnership. We fought constantly and expected to break up every other week. But we did have a few things, things I think you might profit from knowing:

We loved what we did. More than anything. More than sex. Absolutely.

We always felt as if every show was the most important thing in the world, but knew if we bombed, we'd live.

We did not start as friends, but as people who respected and admired each other. Crucial, absolutely crucial for a partnership. As soon as we could afford it, we ceased sharing lodgings. Equally crucial.

We made a solemn vow not to take any job outside of show business. We borrowed money from parents and friends, rather than take that lethal job waiting tables. This forced us to take any job offered to us. Anything. We once did a show in the middle of the Benjamin Franklin Parkway in Philadelphia as part of a fashion show on a hot July night while all around our stage, a race-riot was fully underway. That's how serious we were about our vow.

Get on stage. A lot. Try stuff. Make your best stab and keep stabbing. If it's there in your heart, it will eventually find its way out. Or you will give up and have a prudent, contented life doing something else.

Penn sees things differently from the way I do. But I really feel as if the things we create together are not things we devised, but things we discovered, as if, in some sense, they were always there in us, waiting to be revealed, like the figure of Mercury waiting in a rough lump of marble.

Have heroes outside of magic. Mine are Hitchcock, Poe, Sophocles, Shakespeare, and Bach. You're welcome to borrow them, but you must learn to love them yourself for your own reasons. Then they'll push you in the right direction.

Here's a compositional secret. It's so obvious and simple, you'll say to yourself, "This man is bullshitting me." I am not. This is one of the most fundamental things in all theatrical movie composition and yet magicians know nothing of it. Ready?

Surprise me.

That's it. Place 2 and 2 right in front of my nose, but make me think I'm seeing 5. Then reveal the truth, 4!, and surprise me.

Now, don't underestimate me, like the rest of the magicians of the world. Don't fool yourself into thinking that I've never seen a set of linking rings before and I'll be oh-so-stunned because you can "link" them. Bullshit.

Here's how surprise works. While holding my attention, you withhold basic plot information. Feed it to me little by little. Make me try and figure out what's going on. Tease me in one direction. Throw in a false ending. Then turn it around and flip me over.

I do the old Needle trick. I get a guy up on stage, who examines the needles. I swallow them. He searches my mouth. They're gone. I dismiss him and he leaves the stage. The audience thinks the trick is over. Then I take out the thread. "Haha! Floss!" they exclaim. I eat the floss. Then the wise ones start saying, "Not floss, thread. Thread. Needles. Needles and thread. Ohmygod he's going to thread the need . . . " And by that time they're out and sparkling in the sunshine.

Read Roald Dahl. Watch the old Alfred Hitchcock episodes. Surprise. Withhold information. Make them say, "What the hell's he up to? Where's this going to go?" and don't give them a clue where it's going. And when it finally gets there, let it land. An ending.

It took me eight years (are you listening?) EIGHT YEARS to come up with a way of delivering the Miser's Dream that had surprises and and ENDING.

Love something besides magic, in the arts. Get inspired by a particular poet, film-maker, sculptor, composer. You will never be the first Brian Allen Brushwood of magic if you want to be Penn & Teller. But if you want to be, say, the Salvador Dali of magic, we'll THERE'S an opening.

I should be a film editor. I'm a magician. And if I'm good, it's because I should be a film editor. Bach should have written opera or plays. But instead, he worked in eighteenth-century counterpoint. That's why his counterpoints have so much more point than other contrapuntists. They have passion and plot. Shakespeare, on the other hand, should have been a musician, writing counterpoint. That's why his plays stand out from the others through their plot and music.

I'm tired now. I've been writing to you, my dear bastard son, for 45 minutes merely because, tonight, I'm remembering that evening I first met your mother in Rio, during Carnival . . . ah! . . . and how we loved!

    paternally,
    TELLER

Without a doubt, reading these words set me on the path to where I am today. For anyone wanting to make a living doing something artistic, I hope his words are as helpful to you as they were to me.

Thanks again, Teller

The Human Chimney

IMPRESSIVENESS:
★ ★ ★ ★ ☆

CLASS: OPENER

FACTORS: DANGER, HEALTH, FIRE

REQUIRES: MATCHES, DISREGARD FOR SAFETY

I love this trick, and there's a reason we made it our very first episode of Scam School: it's dead simple, and the effect is amazing. From nowhere, you produce billows of smoke out of your mouth... *it's like you've manufactured smoke in your lungs.*

How It Looks: You strike a match, shake the flame out, and pantomime grabbing a piece of smoke and tossing it into your mouth. After "swallowing" the invisible smoke, you seem to belch up insane amounts of smoke . . . from nowhere.

The Work: Not gonna lie . . . this will probably kill you. You probably shouldn't do it. I'm not any kind of doctor, but I can't imagine any universe in which this is a good idea.

. . . But, if you *are* insane enough to try this, here's how it works: Strike a match, let it burn, and then shake it out. Notice how when

"It's one of the very few effects that you can perform that's MORE impressive when you learn how it's done . . ."

EPISODE

bit.ly/13sdXHA

you strike a match, there's an initial sulfur flash (during which there's very little smoke), followed by a simple burn (during which there's practically NO smoke) . . . and finally, when the match goes out, you see lots of smoke?

Good. That's what your audience will see.

What they *won't* see, is that when you first strike the match, that initial sulfur flash has some kind of vapor (read: "potential poison"), that, when inhaled, will (I kid you not) . . . become **smoke in your freaking lungs**. Read that last sentence again: If you inhale that probably-poisonous-sulfur-whatever-it-is at the exact moment you strike the match, it will become smoke in your lungs.

Right now you should be asking two things:

1. How does it work?

2. Why isn't everyone doing this trick?

The answer to #1 is: "I don't freaking know." It's wizardry as far as I'm concerned. All I know is that when you inhale that crazy sulfur-poison (at least I assume it's poison. I don't really know. In fact, let me reiterate that nobody should do this trick, ever), the invisible gases somehow become smoke inside your lungs. From the different responses I've gotten in humid versus dry climates, I've actually begun to suspect that it has something to do with the water vapor in your lungs . . . like when your breath looks like smoke on a cold, dewy morning.

bit.ly/YKp2QM

DEMONSTRATION

The answer to #2 is: *because it burns like a Muthaf#$%a*. The first time you try this trick, your eyes will water, your nose will sting, and you'll want to freak out . . . be cool. Just act like nothing's wrong and exhale slowly . . . voila! Smoke from nowhere. Once you've practiced this for a few weeks, you'll have it down.

Remember: When you strike the match, make sure it's just a couple inches directly under your nose, and strike right towards your face. Don't worry about burning your face (that'll happen sooner or later no matter what), and whatever you do, don't react to the burning vapors. Just play it cool, relax . . . and exhale.

Oh, and for what it's worth: I've noticed that different colored match heads produce different results. I've found that white or black match heads produce the most smoke, red is fine, and green match heads tend to be the worst. You'll have to experiment yourself to find which ones burn the least for you.

instantly FREEZE a beer

IMPRESSIVENESS:
★★★☆☆

CLASS: TWEENER

FACTORS: DANGEROUS SCIENCE, POSSIBLE EXPLOSIVE GLASS

REQUIRES: BOTTLE OF BEER OR WATER & FREEZER

This one's fun, easy, and best of all, can be done in your own kitchen (plus, you'll actually "fool" yourself). I'm not really sure how to use it to score a drink at the bar, but *damn* does it look cool.

The Setup: Put a few unopened bottles of beer in your freezer for a couple of hours (side note: the visual effect will work best with clear beer bottles, like Corona). When it comes time to remove the beers, you may notice a couple of them have frozen and "exploded," but there should also be a few that are still in a liquid state. Carefully pick these up, set them on the table, and remove the bottle caps.

The Effect: At this point, the trick does itself . . . just give the bottle a good tap on the side of the counter, and as the bubbles start to form, the entire beer will instantly freeze, eventually pushing the ever-expanding ice out the mouth of the bottle.

"There's every possibility that this will explode in your face and you will die . . . By the way, nobody do this. Nobody do this trick! Listen to me, not the words in the book!"

AUDIO

bit.ly/11haPNO

bit.ly/Zioeqd

Why does this work? In a word: supercooling. From the *Concise Dictionary of Science*:

Supercooling: Also known as undercooling, is the process of lowering the temperature of a liquid or a gas below its freezing point without it becoming a solid.

A liquid below its standard freezing point will crystallize in the presence of a seed crystal or nucleus around which a crystal structure can form. However, lacking any such nucleus, the liquid phase can be maintained all the way down to the temperature at which crystal homogeneous nucleation occurs. The homogeneous nucleation can occur above the glass transition where the system is amorphous (non-crystalline) solid."

In the case of our beers, when we strike the bottle, the gas bubbles that form immediately give the supercooled liquid a nucleus around which to freeze. It is possible to supercool water bottles in the same manner, but I've found it much easier with glass bottles of beer than plastic bottles of Diet Coke.

Remember that these are glass bottles filled with a super-cooled liquid, and that water expands as it freezes to ice. I've never seen one of these violently explode, but I suppose it's possible. Make sure you take appropriate safety precautions.

... I'd mention something about kids not trying this, but then I just think *"What kind of idiot gives a bunch of bottles of beer to kids for them to play with?"*

SAFETY NOTE!

4 QUARTERS PUZZLE

"Do not let them off the hook! Let them sit there; let them squirm."

EPISODE

bit.ly/aUYqK9

The Setup: A hard-as-balls puzzle that will drive everyone nuts and hopefully win you some free booze.

The Work: Start out with four quarters set up in a diamond pattern, as seen across the page.

The mark's goal is to get the quarters arranged in a straight line . . . *while following these three rules*:

1. You can only slide one quarter at a time, using only one finger.
2. No picking up, pushing, or stacking of coins (only operate within the two dimensions of the table . . . and no using one coin to push another)
3. Hardest of all: each time you let go of the coin you're moving, *that coin must be touching at least two other coins.*

The Secret: The *real* secret to this trick? The real secret is to wait. Set everything up, tell everyone the rules, and . . . wait. Insist they

keep on trying, and wait as long as it takes. If you've already done an opener like the Human Chimney, then you've captured everyone's attention. This is where you translate that momentum into a free drink. This trick IS SO unbustable, that you can let people work on it all night, until finally, in a fit of desperation, one of them will BEG you for the solution. Tell them that you'll be HAPPY to share the answer with them . . . but you're just . . . so . . . darn . . . thirsty . . .

Before you know it, you'll have a free drink in front of you, and (more importantly) you'll have established a precedent of "pay for play" . . . you'll be happy to keep doing your tricks, as long as the free drinks keep coming.

Don't give up trying to solve this right away! Try it a few times, but if you really can't figure it out, the answer awaits you on the next page.

Don't feel bad if you gave up on this one . . . I did too.

Most people can at least get three of the coins in a row, but get utterly defeated on the fourth . . . and it makes sense, too, right? I mean, how on earth can you add a fourth coin to a row of four, yet have it touch two other coins when you let go?

The answer is in pre-preparing the line of coins. By "walking" out quarters as you see in the illustration, you'll be able to prepare a quarter sized hole in the center of the line . . . everything will fit into place, and you'll secure yourself a tasty frosty beverage.

bit.ly/Y1DOHY

ANSWER DEMONSTRATION

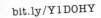

2 pints & a $20

IMPRESSIVENESS:
★ ★ ★ ☆ ☆

CLASS: CLOSER

FACTORS: POTENTIAL MESSES, ELABORATE SETUP, MULTIPLE PHASES

REQUIRES: 2 PINT OR HIGHBALL GLASSES, A $20 BILL, A SINK FULL OF WATER

"Even if the first trick fails, the second one will make you cash."

EPISODE

bit.ly/mARFgL

This two-phase puzzle gives you double the chance to score a free drink . . . and double the chance to make a gigantic mess.

The Work: Next time you're at the bar, grab two highball or pint glasses and a $20 bill. Fold a crease in the bill lengthwise and place it between the glasses as shown, then dunk the whole mess in a sink full of water.

Let the glasses fill up, position them so the rims line up exactly, and when you pull them out, you should have a setup that looks something like the image on the next page.

After that, you're set for two back-to-back challenges:

Challenge #1: See that floating $20 in there? It's all yours if you can remove it without spilling more than a thimbleful of water . . . I'd say "without spilling a drop," but I'm pretty sure that's damn near impossible.

Of course you can touch the glasses, but seriously: 99% of the water that's in there must remain in there the whole time: You can't just grab the glasses and dunk them back in the sink to remove the bill.

Challenge #2: If you're able to get the $20 out, you're perfectly set for a follow-up challenge: Remove all the water from either one of the glasses, WITHOUT touching the glasses, and without touching any objects to the glasses. Oh, and *side note*: no kicking the table or bar to shake the two glasses apart.

For challenge #1, remember that the primary rule is that you can't spill anything (give or take). There's no comment made on what you can use to fish out the bill . . . so take a look in your wallet. Find the most waterproof, thinnest card you can find, and use it like a razor blade to slice right in-between the two glasses. You shouldn't get more than a few drops of leakage, and you'll be able to snag the bill on your way out!

Challenge #2 is a perfect follow-up, not only because of the obvious pre-set of the two glasses, but because a natural side effect of finishing the first challenge will be that the two glasses will be slightly off-center from each other (see picture). As a result, the solution will be to grab a straw, point it right at the biggest gap between the two rims, and then blow as hard as you can. This turbulence will disrupt the water's cohesion and allow all the water from the top glass to pour right out the sides.

Tip: Grab a towel. Or at least think to put the glasses on a large tray to collect all the water!

ANSWER
DEMONSTRATION

bit.ly/YVvowX

Dime in a Bottle

This may be my single favorite combination of bar stunts. Each part is a solid trick on its own, but the combination of the two makes for an awesome one-two punch.

The Setup: Grab an empty wine bottle, drop a dime into it, and replace the cork back in the mouth of the bottle. Push the cork back in so it's flush with the mouth.

The Challenge: Offer a free drink to anyone who can remove the dime from the bottle *first*, and then remove the cork *second*. There's no trick phrasing here: you don't need to smash the bottle, and there won't be any eye-rolling cheesy fake answer at the end. It really can be done, and the solution is immensely satisfying.

bit.ly/11yCRoK   EPISODE

"I'm inordinately proud of dime in the bottle, because I've always experienced both of these effects totally separately, and I thought each of them was kinda weak on their own. But the idea of *combining* them for a one-two punch . . ."

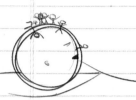

Most people won't be able to figure out even the first half of the scam. And those that do will almost *certainly* be stopped by the second half.

In fact, take a moment to see if you can figure this one out.

Don't worry, I'll wait . . .

Give up? Good. So will your victims.

To Remove the Dime: Grab a spoon and use the handle to jam the cork all the way down into the bottle.

Once the cork is rattling loose inside, it should be simple to shake it and pour out the dime.

This leaves you with the second problem: how to get the cork out of the bottle.

To Remove the Cork: Twist up a cloth napkin and insert it inside the bottle. Tilt the bottle so the cork falls into the folds of the napkin, then carefully begin pulling it out. Once the cork is surrounded on all sides by the napkin, you'll only need to give it a good, solid tug to pull the cork out of the bottle.

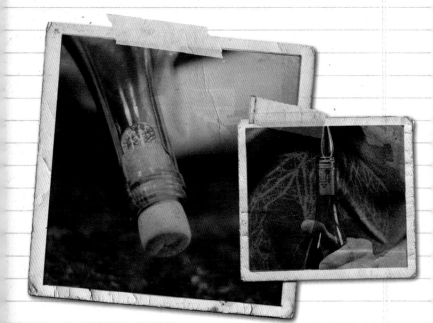

AUDIO
bit.ly/13sfhKj

You're going to want to practice this part before trying it on your friends. There's a bit of a knack to lining up the cork just so. And it's going to take a bit of muscle to yank the cork out, depending on your bottle.

> If you have trouble making it work with the linen napkin, you can also try it with a plastic shopping bag. The thinner material may make it easier to pull the cork through.

DEMONSTRATION

bit.ly/ZlCK1b

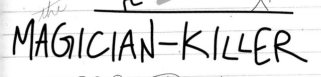

MAGICIAN-KILLER
CARD TRICK

This is a diabolically simple method for a card trick that will fool even seasoned magicians:

How It Looks: You begin by running through the deck, pulling out random cards that you feel a "psychic connection" with. After pulling out 15 to 20 of these cards, they are shuffled, and your subject chooses one and replaces it in the pack. All the psychic cards are then thoroughly shuffled both by you and your target (hell, you can even shuffle all the psychic cards into the plain-jane ones, as well). No matter how well they're shuffled, after you run through the entire deck of cards, you'll know which one belongs to your subject.

"Trust me . . . I didn't think much of it until I saw it performed on magicians and utterly fry them. So if you're a kid and you want to blow away a magician: do this trick. They will *not* suspect it."

EPISODE

bit.ly/13V1U9J

How It's Not Done: There's no sleight-of-hand here. There's nothing to practice. No tricky deck of cards, no secret markings, no hidden accomplices. Everything is done simply and in the open. You can present it as an ESP feat, or (more impressively, I think) a demonstration of your ability to read the facial expressions of your friends.

I originally learned this trick from my uncle when I was in second grade, yet I've seen it fool professional magicians. The method's just too dead-simple, so it flies right under their radar and utterly slays them.

The Secret: It all begins when you pick your "psychic cards." As you look through the deck, you'll notice most of the cards are perfectly symmetrical: they look exactly the same no matter which direction you turn them. There's no "right side up."

bit.ly/12apJ9f

AUDIO

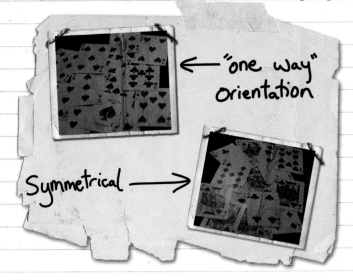

← "one way" orientation

Symmetrical →

However, depending on the design, age, and condition of the deck, you'll be able to find 15-20 cards with a "one way" orientation: cards that can be arranged to have a "right-side-up" and an "upside-down". These will usually be numbered cards in hearts, clubs, and spades (though you can also use the seven of diamonds). Keep an eye out for "natural marks" as well: stuff like a creased corner, a misprinted card, random stains or splotches, even warps in the cards can all be used to give cards an orientation.

As you pull out your psychic cards and place them into a pile, discreetly make sure to orient them all right-side-up (and from now on, make sure not to disturb the orientation when shuffling).

Have a card selected
from the pack, and when
it's returned, make sure
it's in the *reverse*
orientation to the rest
of the pack. Take a look
at this picture, and see if you
can spot the one card reversed from the others:

All of the cards shown have the majority of their pips pointing
upwards. The six of clubs has four pips pointing up, and two pointing
down. The nine of clubs has five pips pointing up, and four pointing
down. Diamonds don't really have a direction to point, but the extra pip
on the seven of diamonds is oriented to be on top. Only the three of
spades is upside-down, with 2 pips pointing down and only 1 pointed up.

With some decks, you can pull the same trick using the designs
on the *back* of the cards, but I don't recommend it. For starters, using
decks with a "one-way back" is a technique very well known to even
amateur magicians, and worse yet: even if they don't know a thing
about magic, it's usually pretty obvious to most people when all the
backs of the cards are arranged the same way except for one.

That's the beauty of this trick: using the orientation of the pips
is so subtle that nobody, not even
magicians, will notice the difference.

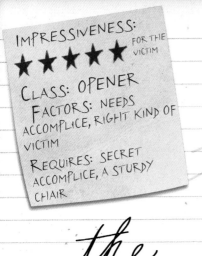

IMPRESSIVENESS: ★★★★★ FOR THE VICTIM

CLASS: OPENER

FACTORS: NEEDS ACCOMPLICE, RIGHT KIND OF VICTIM

REQUIRES: SECRET ACCOMPLICE, A STURDY CHAIR

the L I F T

The Effect: Defying all laws of leverage, you summon a ridiculous amount of strength, lifting your friend at an impossible angle. This one is a win-win . . . the mark gets to experience an absolutely amazing effect while everyone else gets to laugh at the mark.

"I wish in a million years that I could have come up with something as clever as the lift."

EPISODE

bit.ly/YKqEKt

The Work: Start by facing each other. Have the mark hold two arms straight out in front of him. No bend at the elbows, arms parallel to each other and the ground. Step forward and place his arms under your armpits, and ask him to try, as hard as he can, to lift you up off the ground without bending his elbows.

He won't even get close. The leverage is against him, and nobody has enough strength to overcome it. Make sure to give him ample opportunity to make it work ... The more he realizes how impossible the task is, the more amazed he'll be when you pull it off.

bit.ly/ZK5XhZ

AUDIO

Once he's convinced there's no way to lift you, switch positions: place your wrists under his armpits keeping your arms straight and parallel.

> If you really want to throw them for a loop, stand up on a chair to get maximum height. Then you're not just lifting them a few inches, but over a *foot* up into the air.

Take deep breaths, put on a show of summoning all your strength and begin to push upwards. What he *won't* see is one of your friends sneaking up behind him, grabbing your fists, and pushing up on your arms to lift him several inches off the ground. To the mark it is simply as though you got freakishly strong, instantly.

The reactions this effect gets are priceless. Some people will immediately want to try to lift you again, some people will believe you're that strong, and others won't know how to cope.

NIM

246 145 111 123

IMPRESSIVENESS:
★ ★ ☆ ☆ ☆

CLASS: CLOSER

FACTORS: CROOKED GAME

REQUIRES: 17 TOKENS, A SUCKER

This is a game called "Nim," and it's a con-man favorite. There's a million variations, both fair and unfair (and trust me . . . we'll learn a lot of them), but here's a super-simple starting one:

"I don't know if it's going to work at the bar . . . But it is important that you try this scam on your friends, so that you learn the fundamentals for some of the more advanced versions of nim."

EPISODE

bit.ly/11hchyL

Lay down 17 pennies, matches or any other type of tokens. Explain to your friend that you'd like to play a game where each of you take turns removing 1, 2, or 3 pennies from the pile. The object is to NOT take the last penny.

To win, all you need to do is make sure your friend goes first and watch how many pennies he takes:

- If he takes 1, you take 3.

- If he takes 2, you take 2.

- If he takes 3, you take 1.

In other words, for you to win, the total pennies taken each round should be 4.

As long as you follow this rule, you can't lose.

Sooner or later, your mark will get suspicious, and ask YOU to go first . . . no problem: just keep one extra token palmed in your hand the whole time you play. Whenever you go first, reach in and grab a token while you release the one in your palm. Now you've gone first, yet the total count is still 17 tokens (and now it's their turn).

If you want to get maximum enjoyment out of this trick, make sure to lose the first few games when you teach your friend, just to get his confidence up. Later, once he feels comfortable with the game, you can start betting lunches, drinks, or anything else.

bit.ly/12aq2B2

AUDIO

ADVANCED! NIM

IMPRESSIVENESS:

★ ★ ★ ☆ ☆

CLASS: CLOSER

FACTORS: GAME IS MORE FAIR, JUST AS CROOKED

REQUIRES: 15 COUNTERS

Memorize a few configurations, and you'll hold the key to another unbeatable game and loads of free drinks:

I mentioned that Nim is simultaneously totally fair and completely unbeatable. This advanced version of the game is even simpler for the sucker to play, but just as stacked in your favor.

The Rules: Set up three piles of markers, with the starting numbers of 3, 5, and 7. On each player's turn, they can take as many markers as they want from any *one* pile. Whoever takes the last marker loses.

"You should give away the first nim. Tell people how you fooled them, then introduce this as a totally fair way to play from then on . . . THAT'S when you're totally going to screw them out of free beers."

bit.ly/Y1x394   EPISODE

AUDIO

To Win: There are five "pole positions," winning configurations that you can always achieve in just one move (as long as you go second). Once you've hit one of these pole positions, no matter what move they make, you'll always be able to hit the next pole position on your turn. Keep following the pole positions, and you'll be guaranteed to win the game.

You'll have to memorize the winning configurations, but they're easier to remember than it looks (oh, and don't worry about the order of the piles, only the values):

Winning Configurations:

- 1, 2, 3

- 2, 4, 6

- 1, 1, 1

- 1, 4, 5

- . . . or two even piles.

To help remember all the configurations, I just think about guns: The initial setup is 357 (as in the .357 Magnum). The only tricky pole position is 145, so I think of "one colt .45." The rest are super straightforward: 111, 123, 246, and two even piles. When you first start practicing you can use this book as your cheat sheet, but you won't need it for very long.

Remember that once you hit a winning configuration, you'll always be able to continue hitting them. As you near the end of a game, make sure to pay attention: it's easy to get caught up in trying to hit the next pole position and miss an opportunity to win the game.

If you go first, take only one marker. It won't significantly alter the setup, and after their first turn you should be able to hit one of the winning configurations. The only way you'll lose is if they're already hip to this scam and beat you to the punch, hitting all the pole positions (if that happens, team up and take on the rest of the bar).

There have been bajillions of math papers and computer simulations written around different versions of nim, but the first time I saw this take on it was thanks to Opie Houston at the TAOM convention a few years ago. Mega-thanks go to him for suggesting we cover it on *Scam School*.

31
the
ULTIMATE
rigged card game

The Setup: Pull out all the aces, 2's, 3's, 4's, 5's and 6's in a deck of cards and set them into piles by value (a pile of four aces, a pile of four twos, a pile of four threes, etc.).

The Rules: Each player takes a turn picking up a single card and adding it to "the pot," increasing its total amount by the value of each card. The first player to take the pot over 31 loses.

The Trick: As in advanced nim, there are "pole positions" you'll want to reach on your turn: 3, 10, 17, and 24. Once you've hit a pole position, make sure that each following round the total of your draw PLUS the sucker's draw equals 7. This will keep you hitting the pole positions right up until you hit 31.

"Even after you teach them how to win . . . you can STILL beat them!"

bit.ly/17UDrkm

EPISODE

rules: first over 31 <u>LOSES</u>

Pole positions: 3, 10, 17, and 24

The Twist: The best part about this scam is that you can actually teach the whole trick to your sucker and *still* beat him. Explain in detail exactly how you beat him. Let him go first and achieve one of the pole positions (out of the gate, he'll pick a 3). Then continue to burn the same card over and over (keep drawing 4's, which will force him to use up all the 3's). Once he runs out of the right cards, he'll have no way to properly respond to your plays, allowing you to win the game.

AUDIO

bit.ly/15EJGJf

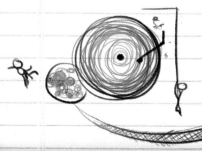

NIM with Nothing

IMPRESSIVENESS:
★★★☆☆

CLASS: TWEENER

FACTORS: ANYTIME, ANYWHERE, PERFECTLY FAIR, TOTALLY RIGGED

REQUIRES: NOTHING (THAT'S THE POINT)

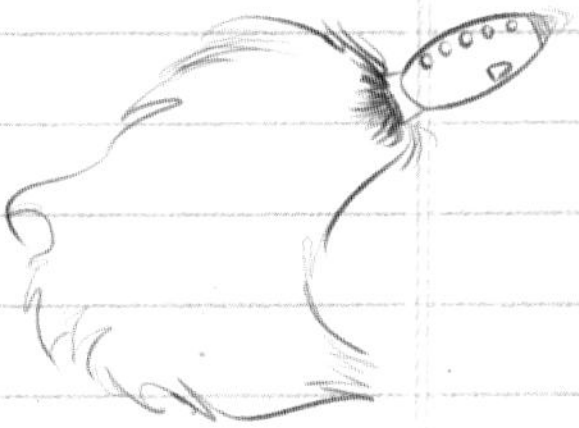

These are fantastic icebreakers, a perfect way to strike up a conversation with someone next to you in line. I recommend that you start by playing the race to 100, then explain it completely (as it's the simpler of the two). Then you can *really* fry 'em with Calendar Nim.

bit.ly/bAiKie

EPISODE

"Separately, they weren't a big deal, but I love the idea that there's a version of nim that can be played with nothing, nothing at all . . . yet you can still cheat."

Before we even begin learning these, I've got to give some mega-thanks to Scott Cram and Lee Blackburn for sending us these crooked games. We've now learned a number of variations of "nim," but none as clever as these two . . . both of which can be played with *no* objects whatsoever.

The Race to 100

The Rules: Starting at 1, players race to hit 100 first by adding any number from 1 to 10 to the current running total. Whoever hits 100 on the nose wins.

The Scam: As with our other version of nim, you can hit "pole positions" that guarantee you a win. In this game, just make sure you add enough to land on 12, 23, 34, 45, 56, 67, 78, and 89. Once you're in the groove, just keep hitting those pole positions and you'll automatically win.

bit.ly/1OwlacS

AUDIO

Calendar Nim

The Rules: Starting at January 1st, players take turns *either* increasing the number of the day, *or* the number of the month (but not both in any one turn). First one to land on December 31st wins.

The Scam: In this case the pole positions are: 1/20, 2/21, 3/22, 4/23, 5/24, 6/25, 7/26, 8/27, 9/28, 10/29, and 11/30. No matter what the other player does, you'll always be able to hit one of these pole positions on your next turn. An easy way to remember the pole positions on calendar nim is to subtract the number of the month from the number of the day . . . you should always get 19.

the RACE

The Challenge: Bet your friend you can drink 2 pints of beer before he can drink 2 shots of his favorite liquor.

Order all the drinks, set them all up side by side and explain there are only a couple of rules: each of you can use only one hand (no double-fisting), nobody can touch each other (no wrestling), and nobody can touch each other's drink glasses (fair enough) . . . oh, and all you need is just a *little* head start. He can't begin his shots until after you've finished your first drink and set the glass on the table. Totally fair, right? Even with the head start, that's still 2 little shots against a whole second pint of beer.

" . . . I learned this much: do not ever, EVER drink with a mission. The night will always end . . . badly."

EPISODE

bit.ly/17fRAY7

If he's still on the fence, offer to make it three *pints* to his two shots. You'll still be able to win.

The Scam: Line up all 4 drinks, and start on your first one. As you drink your pint, your friend will wait and watch anxiously. He'll have his fingers poised to grab the first of his shots. Take your time, drink as slowly as you want, and just before you finish your first pint, remind him that he can't start until you set your glass on the table, and that nobody can touch each other's drink glasses.

Then with a grin, turn your empty pint glass upside down, and set it on the table over his other shot glass. Now he's stuck! He can't touch your glass, and thus can't finish his last shot.

AUDIO

bit.ly/17fRC1Y

three MATCHBOX monte

IMPRESSIVENESS:
★ ★ ☆ ☆ ☆

CLASS: TWEENER

FACTORS: BIG SETUP, EFFECTIVE

REQUIRES: 4 MATCHBOOKS, RUBBER BANDS, GLUE

The 3-card monte's a classic, but it also requires a bit of sleight-of-hand skill. If you're lazy like me, here's a quick-and-dirty way to screw over your friends without learning anything about card manipulation:

The Setup: Set out 3 matchbooks. Pick them up and shake them one at a time to show that two of them are empty, and the third one is clearly full of matches (you can hear them loudly rattling around inside). The challenge is simple: follow the box that's full of matches. Guess correctly, and you win!

"The best magic is the ones where it's not just visual; it's the audio cues that really seduce you."

AUDIO

bit.ly/1Ob1Avg

The Scam: They may get it right the first few times, but as soon as they start placing real money on the table, they won't have a prayer. The gimmick is simple: inside your left-hand sleeve, use a rubber band or tape to attach a fourth, unseen full matchbox. This is the matchbox that will

provide the sound of matches rattling around . . . because all three matchboxes on the table are empty.

When setting up the game, just make sure to pick up and shake the first two matchbooks with your right hand (the one without the secret matchbox). Pick up and shake the third with your left hand, and your secret matchbox will make the rattling sound that "proves" the matchbox is full. From then on, you can always decide who will win, and who will lose, simply by choosing which hand to pick up the matchboxes with.

bit.ly/14M6gk8

DEMONSTRATION

If you want to *really* sell the illusion, use white Elmer's glue to fasten a box-full of matches into a solid block. That way you can even show them the matches inside, then demonstrate the sound of them rattling around. When they successfully pick the right box, shake it around with your ungimmicked hand to show there can't be any matches inside.

3 EGGS 4 $100

I get a lot of emails from Scam School fans. A LOT. But one of my all-time favorites comes from a fan who should have known better:

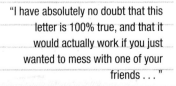

"I have absolutely no doubt that this letter is 100% true, and that it would actually work if you just wanted to mess with one of your friends . . ."

My heat is unBEARable!

bit.ly/1lyESkJ

AUDIO

Hey Brian,

It's been a while! Good to see you're still hard at it with Scam School.

As you say, most of these scams come round again and again in different forms.

Here's a cool twist on an old scam. I paid the messy price (on video) the other day when my uncles laid out the following proposal:

'If we can crack open three eggs on your head, we will pay you $100 EACH. You can either agree or refuse the bet - but if you agree, and then hesitate or back out, you pay us $10 each. Deal?'

Have a think about that for a minute . . . $100, for three eggs? They even said they'd allow me a change of clothes nearby, and a hosing down outside to remove the egg afterwards. Easy money!

This one had me hooked, as I'd never heard anything like it before, and I know a LOT of bar scams, mainly through Scam School and The Real Hustle UK. I knew there had to be a catch. I remembered the old cider in the ear quotation. I know that there's a sucker born every minute. I know that if it looks (or sounds) too good to be true, then it probably is. But I had to know the answer! After a minute's frantic deliberation, I agreed to the deal, knowing that, somehow, I would soon be no better off financially AND covered in egg, to boot.

The conclusion: After agreeing and taking my seat outside, my uncles each cracked open an egg on my head with a big smile, and let it dribble down my face and chin.

After holding the third egg and contemplating it for a moment, the first uncle then handed me the final egg, and wandered off. 'That was FUN!' I heard him saying to his brother as they walked away. I threw the final egg at him, but it bounced off, still whole, and broke on the ground at his feet. Bastards!

Another cool idea for a Scam School episode maybe?

When I recover the clip from my camcorder (I lent it to a friend) I'll stick it up on Facebook and give you a heads-up.

Take it easy,
Cowboy

That "cider quote" he mentioned? It's a classic from *Guys & Dolls*:

"One of these days in your travels, a guy is going to show you a brand-new deck of cards on which the seal is not yet broken. Then this guy is going to offer to bet you that he can make the jack of spades jump out of this brand-new deck of cards and squirt cider in your ear. But, son, do not accept this bet, because as sure as you stand there, you're going to wind up with an ear full of cider."

—Sky Masterson

VS

IMPRESSIVENESS:
★ ★ ★ ★ ☆

CLASS: CLOSER

FACTORS: BIG SETUP, SLOW PAYOFF, IMPRESSIVE VISUAL

REQUIRES: 1 SHOT WHISKEY, 1 SHOT WATER (BOTH FULL TO RIM)

This simple play on high school physics is gorgeous to watch, simple to perform, and sounds utterly impossible:

The Setup: Pour a shot of whiskey (all the way to the rim), and set it next to a shot of water (also filled to the rim). Challenge your friend to figure out a way to get all the whiskey into the water glass, and vice versa, without using a third vessel of any kind (including your mouth).

"Even though it's a simple idea, it's something that's complicated enough that a lot of people won't bother to try it at the bar . . . I'm going to say this: go ahead and try it, because the effect is *way* worth it."

EPISODE

bit.ly/Y1xMXS

The Trick: Whiskey is lighter than water (the better the whiskey, the better this works). Place a playing card over the water-filled shot glass, turn it upside down and place it on top of the whiskey glass. Then, pull the playing card out *just the tiniest amount*, so a small crack opens between the two glasses . . . and wait.

The lighter whiskey will slowly trickle upwards to the top of the water's shot glass, while the water trickles down. It's a really neat looking effect. After 3 to 5 minutes, the two drinks will have completely swapped places.

This is one I highly recommend you practice beforehand. There's no tricky moves to it, but it's easy to make a mess . . . and the cleaner the effect is, the better it's going to look. I mean, if you're dribbling water everywhere and making a mess, you just won't look cool, right?

DEMONSTRATION

bit.ly/1Ob1UKz

AUDIO

bit.ly/1OwlM1V

M!XƎD dRIИKS

The Setup: Lay out six shot glasses in a row and fill every other one with whiskey as shown.

The Challenge: End up with all six glasses in a row, but with three shots of whiskey on one side, and three empty shot glasses on the other . . . *and do it by touching the fewest possible glasses.*

AUDIO

"Sometimes you need material just to have more material. But this is one you should know, if for no other reason than because somebody will try to pull it on you at some point."

bit.ly/10blW57

setup: ⬛🥃🥃🥃🥃🥃

goal: 🥃⬛🥃⬛🥃⬛

Now, the phrasing of "the fewest possible glasses" is important. It's ambiguous: I mean after all . . . how many is *the fewest*? is 3 few enough? Is there a way to only touch 2? *Wait-a-minute . . . is there a way to touch ZERO glasses? LESS than zero???*

It's this kind of self-doubt that will drive people crazy. Either they'll be over-confident and convinced their solution touches the fewest, or they'll be convinced that no matter what they've done, there has to be *at least one more glass they can cut* . . .

The Answer: The trap here is that most people think in terms of swapping around shot glasses, and they'll be certain that you can't do it touching fewer than two. But remember that you said nothing about "swapping glasses." All you want is the six glasses in a row, with every other glass filled with whiskey . . .

. . . which is why all you need to do is pick up the last whiskey on the right side, and pour its contents into the only empty glass on the left side. Set the newly-emptied shot glass back in its original position, and collect your free drink.

Quicksilver MATCHES

IMPRESSIVENESS:
★ ★ ★ ★ ☆

CLASS: OPENER

FACTORS: OPTIONAL
PRE-SET GIMMICK

REQUIRES: 2
MATCHBOOKS

The Effect: Taking two matches from different matchbooks (one black, one brown), you cause them to visibly switch places, right under their eyes. This one plays best as a small, impromptu effect, and in the right situation I've had people audibly *gasp* when they see the transposition.

The Method: For this you'll need to find a few books of black paper matches. Most black books of matches have a dark, colored side and a light, uncolored side. You *can* do the trick with just two matches from the same matchbook, but to really sell the illusion you'll want it to look as though each match came from a different matchbook.

"In order to do it completely right, you're going to have to do some prep work . . ."

EPISODE

bit.ly/13sgTno

bit.ly/17UE2lZ

AUDIO

If you remove the entire block of matches from a black-colored matchbook, reverse them, and staple them into the cover of another brand, you'll have a convincing display of what appears to be one book of all-black matches, and another book of all-uncolored matches.

Before you perform the effect, you're going to need to learn a tricky move: Start by holding the match by the match-head between your thumb and forefinger. Roll the match back and forth, and you should be able to feel a "pop" sensation as it quickly flips from one side to the other. The tighter you squeeze and turn, the faster and more precise that "pop-move" will feel.

Now practice executing that pop-move at the exact same time you turn over your hand, as if you're showing the other side of the match. When properly executed, it will look like you're displaying both sides of the match to be either black or cardboard-colored.

bit.ly/12as6ZR

WATCH THIS SUPER-IMPORTANT DEMONSTRATION TO SEE IT IN ACTION!

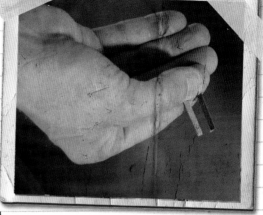

Once you have this down, practice pinching two matches at the same time, side-by-side. The effect is exactly the same, but it seems like it would be even more impossible for you to be performing any sleight-of-hand.

Essentially, you're always showing the same side of both matches twice, but it looks like both sides are being shown.

In performance, pull out both matches, show "both" sides, then quickly execute the pop-move as you shake your hand. To your friend, the matches will have instantly changed places.

Magicians call this technique the "paddle move," and it's easily one of the most visual, simple effects in magic. Once you have it down, you'll find that the extra step of pre-setting up the matchbooks is well worth your time and effort.

CLOSE-UP DEMONSTRATION OF
THE POP-MOVE TECHNIQUE

bit.ly/17fShRd

THE KEY CARD

AUDIO

bit.ly/ZlFpYM

IMPRESSIVENESS:

★ ★ ★ ★ ☆

CLASS: TWEENER/CLOSER

FACTORS: MORE COMPLEX TRICK, BIG PAYOFF

REQUIRES: DECK OF CARDS

This card trick is quite possibly responsible for more free beers than any other in history. It's not just a magic trick, it's a cleverly-laid trap *guaranteed* to win you a frosty cold one.

Here's How It Plays Out: Have your friend freely choose a card and place it on top of the deck. Then lose the card in the center by taking turns with your friend repeatedly cutting the deck, then completing the cut. When both of you are confident that neither of you knows where the card is, begin dealing the cards face up on the table.

Long *after* your friend's card has been dealt face up on the table, you hold out the next card in the deck (which clearly can't be his

"This is, without a doubt, THE trick that caused me to become a magician . . ."

EPISODE

bit.ly/12F8JsW

card, since he can see his card staring him in the face on the table) and ask your friend "How much do you want to bet that the *next card I turn over* will be your card?" You'll be surprised by how much he offers . . . . He thinks you've already messed up the trick!

But imagine his surprise when you replace the card you're holding back into the deck and instead *turn over his face up card on the table*!

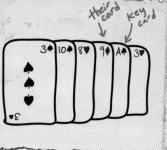

their card   key card

3♠ 10♠ 8♥ 9♦ A♦ 3♥

The Secret: Before starting, find out what card is on the bottom of the deck. For this explanation, we'll say it's the ace of spades. When you cut his card into the deck, the Ace of Spades will now be right on top of it. No matter how many times you cut the cards, the Ace will always be on top of his card (even if you happen to cut between the ace and his card, the very next cut will place the two right back next to each other).

When you deal the cards face up onto the table, notice which card comes *after* the Ace: that's his card. Take note of it, but keep dealing like you didn't notice a thing. As you continue to deal, make sure you don't cover up his card. You want him to be 100% certain that you've totally missed it.

And now for my favorite subtlety: at the exact moment you say "How much do you want to bet that the next card I turn over will be your card . . ." use your index finger to flick the card that's in your hand. This little audio cue makes it perfectly clear that the card you're talking about *must* be the card in your hand . . . right? This is a fantastic moment where you lie without words. It's this little misdirection that seals the deal and guarantees you the win.

bit.ly/1lyFIxX   DEMONSTRATION

CHEESY BEER gags

IMPRESSIVENESS:

★★★★☆ – ★★★★★☆

CLASS: TWEENERS

FACTORS: EACH GAG NEEDS TO WAIT FOR THE RIGHT MOMENT

REQUIRES: BOTTLE OF BEER

If you've ever watched Scam School, you know we pride ourselves on giving you only the very best bar scams . . . but in this chapter, we break our streak and instead present you with four stupid beer gags.

Yes, they're stupid, but they're also awesome.

The Eye of Hercules: This one actually fools people, but it's so simple that most people write it off. To make it look like you're opening a beer with your eye, remove the bottle cap and set it gently on top of the beer. Wait until your mark is watching, then place the bottle in your eye socket and turn the beer as you mime opening the bottle with your eye. Here's the kicker though: as you do this, make a hissing "Ssssss" sound with your mouth. If you get the sound and acting right, they'll be convinced you just opened the twist-off bottle with your eye.

And shut up: it *does so* fool people.

bit.ly/12atcVs

EPISODE

"Shut up. I know what you're about to say: 'Dude, these are totally cheesy and they're dumb.' Yes. They are, AND THEY'RE AWESOME."

AUDIO

The Overflow: This is a gag everyone falls for, *exactly once*. If you're the first one to perform it on someone, you can be the jerk he'll remember forever. With two just-opened beer bottles, move to toast your friend, but instead tap your full beer firmly on the mouth of his bottle. Give it a good rap but don't break anything. For a few seconds, nothing will happen . . . and then his beer will overflow with foam.

The Levitation: This gag seems to impress the performer more than the audience. I'm not even sure why it fools anyone, but it does look cool and it's fun to do.

EYE OF HERCULES
DEMONSTRATION

Wipe down to dry an empty beer or wine bottle and set it upside down on the bar. If you set your index finger on top of the bottle while your thumb pinches in from the side, you can create the loose illusion of the bottle having become stuck to your middle finger.

OVERFLOW
DEMONSTRATION

LEVITATION DEMONSTRATION

bit.ly/12atM5H

I honestly don't know if this is any kind of "fooler" effect, but I find myself doing it every time I'm at the bar.

Stealing the Dollar: Again, this one's an entry-level gag, but one that everyone loves to play. Set a dollar bill underneath an inverted beer bottle, and announce that anyone can keep the dollar if he can get it out from underneath the bottle without letting the bottle tip over.

The rules are: No touching the bottle, and no use of any other objects.

Once they give up, show that by carefully rolling the bill, the bill itself can push the bottle off the edge, and get you the bill, scott free.

STEALING THE DOLLAR DEMONSTRATION

bit.ly/ZiqzBo

jumping egg

The Setup: Grab two 1-oz shot glasses, set them side-by-side, and place an egg in one of them. The challenge is to get the egg out of the first shot glass and into the second one . . . without touching *anything*. And "not touching anything" really means just that: no touching the glasses, no using a straw to poke stuff, no banging on the table to make everything bounce around (and by the way, prepare for your mark to attempt all of these). In this challenge, touching nothing means *touching nothing*.

bit.ly/xZSJyZ

EPISODE

Here's a quick, simple challenge with a surprising, visual payoff:

Make sure you practice this beforehand, and make sure you're using 1-ounce shot glasses. Many of the more popular tourist shot glasses are too big: the egg sits too deeply in them, and can't be blown out at any strength.

JUMPING EGG

bit.ly/ZlGzUe

AUDIO

DEMONSTRATION

bit.ly/YKuQde

The Method: This doesn't seem like it'll work, but if you lean in close and give a sharp, percussive blow at the outer edge of the egg, your breath will blast the egg out of the first shot glass and directly into the opposite one. I love this reveal because not only is it counter-intuitive, but actually looks magical to watch. Even if your mark suspects the answer has something to do with blowing, they'll usually just waste their efforts with big, long gasps of air that'll will do nothing but move the shot glasses around.

IMPRESSIVENESS:
★ ★ ★ ★ ☆
CLASS: CLOSER
FACTORS: COMPLICATED
EXECUTION, NEEDS PRACTICE

REQUIRES: 3 PENNIES,
2 DIMES

This is the perfect closer for a set of scams at the bar . . . It's simple to set up, hard as hell to figure out, and most amazingly: it's one of the rare puzzles that you can show the correct answer, yet *still* fool them.

The Setup: Place 2 dimes and 3 pennies in a line in this order: PENNY DIME PENNY DIME PENNY.

The Goal: Arrange the coins in a line, with all the pennies on one side and all the dimes on another.

The Rules: You can only move 2 coins at a time, and each time you make a move, you must move both a currently-touching penny and a dime (11 cents). Each time you let go of the coins, they must be along the same line as the original setup, and (of course) you can't use any coins to push any other coins around.

Start
(P) (d) (P) (d) (P)

goal
(d) (d) (P) (P) (P)

AUDIO
bit.ly/17UELn8

EPISODE

bit.ly/9ORC9I

"The #1 thing we learned while shooting the 11-cent slide . . . is that it's hard as hell to tell the difference between pennies and dimes in a darkened bar."

The Twist: There are actually two ways to solve this puzzle, and you can even show one of the solutions to your mark . . . and they *still* won't be able to reproduce it. This means you can set up the puzzle, let them give up, and then offer them a double-or-nothing chance to solve the puzzle, after you've given them the answer.

Don't think this sounds too difficult? Go ahead and try it out.

The Answer: For the 5-move solution, just memorize the phrase "Over, over, half-over, swap, obvious." If you can remember that, you'll know to execute the following moves:

11 CENT SLIDE
5-MOVE SOLUTION

bit.ly/ZGntGQ

move 1: "over"

move 2: "over" again

move 3: "half-over" means take these two out of the middle

move 4: "swap" means to complete the switch here

move 5: . . . and finally, the last move should be obvious as it completes the puzzle.

Practice a few times so you can execute the move quickly enough that your sucker will have a hard time following along.

. . . if they insist on seeing the answer again, oblige them by solving the puzzle a slightly *different* way this time, with the 4-move answer. For this version, just remember "Big over, big over, swap, obvious." The moves go:

> move 1: "big over" means moving them over, with extra room for 11 cents in the middle.
>
> move 2: "big over" again means a big jump to the right.
>
> move 3: "swap" means to complete the switch here (just like before)
>
> move 4: "obvious" and again, the last move should be obvious.

You should be able to pick up double the drinks with this scam . . . set up the original puzzle and let them go nuts trying to solve it. Right when it looks like they're going to give up, offer them a deal: if they're willing to go double-or-nothing, you will full-on show them the answer . . . they only need to be able to replicate your results.

. . . Amazingly, they won't have a prayer.

4-MOVE SOLUTION
DESCRIPTION

bit.ly/15F5tka

Setup: P1 d1 P2 d2 P3

1. P1 d1 P2 d2 P3   P1 d1

2. P2 d2 P3   P1 d1 P2 d2

3. P3 d1 P2 P1 d1 P2 d2

4. P2 P1 P3 d1 d2

STRENGTH school

Psst ... want the secret to becoming the WORLD'S STRONGEST MAN?
You Do? Sweet.
The secret is ...
... hard work and years of training.

I know. It's disappointing. But that's only because you asked the wrong question:

If you were crafty enough to ask "What's the secret to *looking* like the world's strongest man, but without any actual training or effort?" then you, my friend would have what it takes to enter our version of "Strength School."

1- bit.ly/1Ownv7w
2- bit.ly/17Nm165
3- bit.ly/11hfYoj
4- bit.ly/ZiqWvI

ALL FOUR STRENGTH SCHOOL EPISODES

1   2   3   4

"He will flex his forearm muscle, and you will touch it ... and it will *feel like a bar of iron.*"

Some of my favorite episodes of Scam School were when we taught you to *fake* your way into (almost) duplicating the feats of the world's strongest men. Our guest co-host and teacher was a former world-champion arm wrestler and 100% genuine strongman: Dennis Rogers. Dennis has appeared on dozens of TV shows, holds numerous world records, and has been called "pound for pound, the world's strongest man."

. . . and lucky for us, he gets ticked off by all the strong-man fakers out there. Ticked off enough to share the secrets used by cheaters to *fake* authentic strongman feats.

If you haven't seen these episodes already, they're definitely worth checking out. Dennis's talent and strength is truly amazing.

HOW TO RIP A PHONEBOOK IN HALF

So in one of my favorite episodes, Dennis taught us a few tricks to tear phone books and decks of playing cards in half by baking them in an oven, to make them more brittle. We grabbed two

phone books and a few decks of cards, threw them in the oven, and baked them for about 40 minutes at 400 degrees Fahrenheit. After their time in the heated oven, the cards were made much more brittle, so that folding them in half would cause them not to bend or crease, but simply snap in two like a twig.

Even after the cards and phone book were brittleized (yes, that's a real word . . . look it up in the 'shwoodtionary), I still needed to use proper tearing technique to get them to snap in half. And for that, it's important to think of your grip on the cards as serving only one purpose: to keep them in a solid block. If your grip can keep the cards or phonebook as a solid block, you should be able to use a hard twisting motion to start tearing through the cards. As you continue twisting each of your hands in a different direction, the block of cards/phonebook should tear right in half.

The amazing part of this is that after a few practice runs with the baked cards, you'll find that you understand the leverage well enough that you can actually tear a real, unprepared deck of cards.

BEND A NAIL OR WRENCH WITH YOUR HANDS

We also learned how to cheat and "steal leverage" to bend a large nail. We sewed a pair of "cheater pipes" into some standard work gloves: simple, hollow steel pipes placed right along the palm of each hand, with a hole just inside of the thumb on each glove. To set up your bend, explain you're going to do the impossible: bend an 8-inch, heavy-duty spike with nothing but your own strength.

You can even start acting like you're about to do it with your bare hands, but then pause and explain that you ought to wear some safety gloves to keep from messing up your hands.

When you put on the gloves, insert each end of the spike into the empty hollow of each cheater pipe, and you'll discover 2 things: (1) in this setup, you're no longer bending an 8-inch spike, but a structure over a foot long, giving you much more leverage, and (2) the gaps in the pipes slightly change the angles of the bend, essentially giving you a "head start" on beginning the bend, which is usually the hardest part.

It'll take a little effort to set up your gloves, but *man* will this one impress people.

BEND A FRYING PAN AND A HORSESHOE WITH YOUR BARE HANDS

Remember, there's two ways to fake feats of strength: by using leverage to amplify your own strength, or by weakening the object to be manipulated. To roll up a frying pan, hit up the dollar store. You should be able to find a super-flimsy pan for just a couple of

bucks. As long as you don't let anyone inspect them up close before the bend, it should look pretty impressive when you roll it up.

A horseshoe will do a much better job at convincing someone you have actual strength. Start with a genuine horseshoe and use an angle grinder to grind down the center until it gets so thin you can comfortably bend it. Conceal your work with a few strokes of paint, and the end result should be a heavy horseshoe that you can hand out for inspection. It'll feel heavy and solid, yet you'll be able to bend it with your own bare hands.

THE HUMAN LINK/TUG OF WAR:

When Dennis performs it, this is a true feat of nothing but pure grip strength: two iron triangles with ropes attached are held tightly in his hands as two volunteers pull with all their strength in opposite directions. Amazingly he's got the goods to keep them from breaking his grip . . . and it's not even a cheat. Dennis has even performed a version of this trick holding back *four Harley-Davidson motorcycles*, pulling in opposite directions. Hell, he's also done this preventing two *airplanes* attempting to take off in different directions.

Read that last sentence again, then re-evaluate your life.

To *cheat* our way to duplicating the effect, we crafted similar-looking triangles, but with an important difference: ours had a welded peg-and-hole design that allowed us to physically link the two handles, which meant I never had to even flex a muscle.

Fists of Fury: This one's super easy, and you can do it immediately. Ask a friend to hold their arms out straight in front of them, with hands balled into fists placed vertically, one atop the other. Challenge them to use their strength to resist you knocking their fists off of each other, then use just a couple of fingers to slap their fists in opposite directions. The leverage is so far against them that they won't be able to hold back.

holding thumb

The leverage is so awkward that even *I* could knock Dennis's hands off each other.

To reverse the scam, set up your fists in what looks like the same way, but with one major difference: extend your thumb from your lower fist and wrap your upper fist around it. Now it'll look the same, but there's no possible way he can knock your fists apart.

Payback: Here's a quick way to get the drop on a friend and *slap the hell out of him*. Tell him you've got something to show him, and then have him hold up 2 fingers on each hand (like he's giving two peace signs). Have him nestle all 4 fingers together as shown . . .

. . . then with your left hand, grab all four fingers tightly as you start slapping him around with your right. The combined friction and leverage will keep his hand bound and he'll be helpless to stop you.

Oh, also: run.

The Ultimate Setup: This one's a classic bar stunt of strength: Announce you're going to prove that you are stronger than everyone else in the room, *combined*. To prove it, walk up to a wall and place both your palms on it. Then have everyone else in the room line up behind you, each placing his hands on the shoulders of the person in front of him. As one big line, the challenge is to use their combined strength to push you up against the wall . . . and amazingly, *they won't be able to do it.*

This one is partly due to leverage, but mostly because the strength of each person is lost on whoever they're leaning against. Because just as each person is pushing forward, they're also pushing *backwards* against the person behind them. The net effect is that you really are only resisting the person directly behind you — everyone else just resists each other.

PENNIES for a PINT

IMPRESSIVENESS:
★ ★ ★ ★ ★

CLASS: CLOSER

FACTORS: REQUIRES PRE-SET GIMMICK TO BE CARRIED

REQUIRES: PENNIES, TIN SNIPS

No matter what the setup, the very best scams are the ones that let the mark think they're on top, only to get punked in the end. That's what makes the penny prediction so great.

The Setup: Reach into your pocket and pull out a bunch of change. Announce that you're going to make a prediction using a few pennies. After a bit of shuffling, close your fist around your prediction and ask your mark to think of any two-digit number from 1 to 100. Once they're ready, have them perform the following simple calculations *without* showing you any of their work:

- start with their two-digit number

- add up the two digits of their number, and subtract that amount from their number

- add up the digits that make up this new number

- divide that sum by two

bit.ly/17NmGEQ

EPISODE

"This is the first trick you're going to learn that requires you to keep something on you to prepare for the occasion. What does it take to keep a few half-pennies in your pocket? It's totally worth it, and the effect blows them away."

To clarify, imagine they had picked the number 62. Here's what they'd do:

- start with their two-digit number: (62)

- add up the two digits of their number (6+2=8), and subtract that amount from their number (62-8=54)

- add up the digits that make up this new number (5+4=9)

- divide that sum by two (9/2=4.5)

Now imagine your mark's surprise when you bet him a beer that whatever final number they came up with will match the prediction pennies in your hand. They'll be convinced that your trick didn't work and that they've got themselves a free beer coming. I mean, seriously: there's no way you can have 4.5 pennies in your fist, right?

Then imagine their shock when you open your fist and show you're holding four and a HALF pennies. Zing!

The Work: The math takes care of itself. As long as you follow the above directions, the end result number will always be 4.5. To make the half penny, use some tin snips, garden shears, or a good pair of scissors.

My suggestion is to make a few half pennies and keep 'em in your pocket for just the right moment. After all, what's it take to keep a half penny on you, and how great is it to stick it to a good mark?

This trick came to us from the genius wizardry of "Diamond" Jim Tyler and his awesome "Bamboozlers" book series.

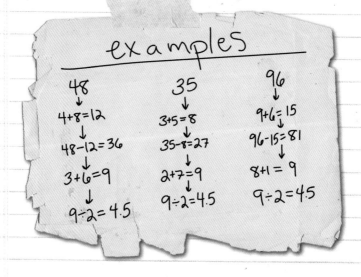

examples

48
↓
$4+8=12$
↓
$48-12=36$
↓
$3+6=9$
↓
$9÷2=4.5$

35
↓
$3+5=8$
↓
$35-8=27$
↓
$2+7=9$
↓
$9÷2=4.5$

96
↓
$9+6=15$
↓
$96-15=81$
↓
$8+1=9$
↓
$9÷2=4.5$

SHORT CHANGE

IMPRESSIVENESS: ☆☆☆☆☆

CLASS: CRIME

FACTORS: SERIOUSLY, THIS IS A CRIME

REQUIRES: THE BALLS TO COMMIT A CRIME

EPISODE

bit.ly/13Vb8m8

We're turning to the dark side and learning actual crime. Remember, the following is for *INFORMATIONAL AND ENTERTAINMENT PURPOSES ONLY*!

Everyone's heard the term "short change," but very few people know about the actual street con for which it's named. This scam is performed thousands of times each year, and con men score millions of dollars just by using a few simple verbal tricks . . .

"Freaking short change . . . this one is near and dear to my heart, because I got conned for $50 of the movie theater's money when I was in high school . . ."

bit.ly/XTDc4P

AUDIO

DEMONSTRATION OF A SIMPLE SHORTCHANGE

The Goal: To get more money out of the register than you're entitled to, without the attendant even realizing it.

The Method: In the chapter, we're presenting one of the simplest versions of the short change. Advanced versions of this scam can take people for hundreds of dollars. This version uses three phases:

Phase I:

Start by performing some kind of fair trade to get the register open. You can ask for change for a twenty (looking for a ten, a five, and five ones), or maybe buy an item and pay with a large bill (for example, buy a beer with a twenty, giving you the drink, and $15 change). It doesn't matter. All that matters is that you start with a fair trade that involves a lot of bills. This gets the register open and the attendant's head filled with a bunch of numbers, which sets you up for . . .

Phase II: The Second Layer

This is a trade you'll start on top of the first one. It's a trade that's *almost* fair, but involves a mistake that makes the short change possible. In our example, while the till is still open, explain how you have some $1 bills to get rid of and that you'd like to trade a bunch of them for a $10. Drop down a stack of $1 bills (actually containing only 9 of them) and scoop up their $10 bill (along with the change from phase one). Remind the cashier to count those bills and "make sure it's right" (again, this fills the cashier's head with more numbers and builds some time delay).

After the count, they'll notice that your amount is wrong. In this case, we're short $1. In alternate versions, you could have overpaid, or maybe the last bill was a five instead of a one. It doesn't matter what's wrong with the money you provide: what matters is that the distraction allows you to "correct" the mistake and grab more of the register's cash, using . . .

Phase III: The Correction

Now if you were playing fair in the $9 example above, you'd correct it simply by giving them another dollar . . . but that's not what you'll do. Instead, you'll say, "Wait . . . I don't want to get confused here . . . We've got nine, right? So let's make that ten . . . Oh, and I've got some more ones here . . . We'll make it 10, 11, 12, 13, 14, 15 . . . and 5 dollars more will make it twenty. We'll just trade for my original twenty instead."

Did you catch it? By using time delay, multiple numbers, and a reference back to "the original twenty," we essentially use our stack of nine $1 bills *twice*. First to trade for a $10 bill, then again (added with more money) to trade for a $20.

The MIRROR

The Work: For this effect I've dressed up a straight-up old school bar scam with a newfangled presentation. Here's my simple presentation for the classic "you do as I do."

The Setup: Bet your friend that he can't copy everything you do. In other words, he needs to act as a mirror image of you, copying every move in as close to real-time as possible. Don't worry: you're not going to make any crazy-fast moves to try to trip him up. You're going to move slowly and simply at all times . . . in theory, he should have no trouble following along.

EPISODE

"When I was a kid I loved it, but I had never figured out a way to give it personality . . ."

bit.ly/11hgQtOt

The Steps: You'll come up with your own presentation for this, and add your own bits of business, but the main beats are:

1. Both of you take a drink.

2. Hold your drink forward in a toast. He does the same.

3. You take a drink. So does he.

4. You toast again. He does, too.

5. Finally, you spit a mouthful of your drink back into your glass. He can't . . . *because he's already swallowed.*

Now, remember: the more you dress up the presentation with red herrings, the greater chance they'll miss your mouthful of drink.

That's why I frame this as a "mirror image" game . . . I fuss over the glasses, the napkins, the drink positions, setting everything at the table up to make a perfect mirror image. Then I explain they must copy me in as close to real-time as possible. Once we start, I add an important subtlety: after the first drink, I have them repeat

bit.ly/11yHAXE

AUDIO

whatever I say. That reinforces the point that we've both swallowed our drinks. Because of that reinforcement, the second time you start the ritual, your sucker will think he's about to say something, guaranteeing he swallows first (and ends up owing you a drink).

Advanced Follow-Up: Since this bar scam's been around for so long, you may run into someone who has heard of it before. As insurance, whenever you spit your drink back into the glass, always retain about half of the liquid in your mouth . . . that way, if some wise-ass spits his mouthful back into the glass, you can wipe that smug grin off his face by spitting another mouthful into your beer.

Don't Forget

we must find a way back to Universe X

X-RAY EYES

EPISODE

"There's a few lessons we've had to learn with Scam School over the years, and one of them is 'putting the method to a trick in the title is a TERRIBLE IDEA.'"

bit.ly/15EQh6E

This is one of the simplest, most versatile tricks in this book. You can play it as a demonstration of supernatural abilities, a show of luck, or a test of your keen senses. It's perfect because it forces your audience to focus obsessively on all the wrong things, which only makes the effect more powerful.

bit.ly/XTDAAq

AUDIO

The Scene: Lay out five quarters in criss-cross formation (similar to the layout of the 5 pips on on the "5" side of a die), and cover them with five bottle caps. Announce that as a result of being struck by radioactive lightning, you now have perfect vision and a photographic memory (just go with it). To demonstrate your talents, turn around and invite your friend to steal one of the quarters you've covered up and replace the bottle cap exactly back in place. Make sure they do their best to make it look like absolutely nothing has changed. Yet when you turn back around, using nothing but your incredible powers of perception, you'll correctly identify which bottle cap was robbed.

   And you'll *keep* doing it. As many times as they want. The more they watch you, the more impossible the trick will seem. They'll insist on covering your eyes. They'll cover your ears. They'll try to trick you by switching around the bottle caps. None of these will foil you. You'll always make the correct identification.

The Method: You have a secret assistant on your side. Before your friends show up, make friends with the guy next to you at the bar. Buy him a drink and teach him a simple code: when a bottle cap is robbed, have him indicate which one is missing a quarter by placing his drink on the corresponding position on his napkin.

If you don't want to go meeting strangers at a bar, you can just as easily pre-arrange something like this with one your friends. But remember that the strength of this scam is that there doesn't appear to be *any* connection between you and the random guy drinking next to you. If people know that you have a connection to other people watching, they're going to be much more likely to suspect a secret assistant or code.

napkin

Caps

CaRD swAp

IMPRESSIVENESS:
★★★★☆

CLASS: TWEENER

FACTORS: LOGIC, RIGGED GAME

REQUIRES: DECK OF CARDS

This game is evil. It's evil and it means you malice. Why else would a game look so completely honest and fair . . . yet prove that your skills mean **absolutely nothing**.

The Setup: Lay 13 cards of one suit in a row, from ace to king. Below, lay 13 more cards in the reverse direction, from king to ace.

"For this one, I recommend let your friends play. Do not play yourself."

bit.ly/9ZZ59F

EPISODE

The Game: Each turn, a player can swap any two cards they like from the bottom row (The top layer of cards are never moved; they're set there just to number the positions).

BUT, whenever a card from the bottom layer lines up with its match on the top layer, that card is "locked in" and cannot be moved again (indicate this by flipping the card face down). To illustrate this point, before the match even begins, make sure to flip over the 7, as it's already in its matching spot. During play, players take turns back and forth, and the winner is the LAST one to lock in a card.

Fair enough, right?

I recommend you explain this game to two friends and have them play multiple games against each other. Remind them that the winner of each game has honors to go first in the following game.

AUDIO

bit.ly/ZlIMyP

They'll come up with all kinds of theories as to why they're winning or losing. They'll insist they've got the strategy figured out . . . yet when you join the game, you'll be absolutely, positively, 100% guaranteed to win your match.

Why?

The Reveal: Because no matter what your strategy, no matter how you play, no matter what you do . . . whoever goes first, will lose.

Always.

That's the beauty of insisting that the winner goes first . . . it will force all players into a back-and-forth of wins and losses, convincing them that there's a real technique to the match . . .

Which is how you'll be able to step in, go second, and win when it counts.

tie your friend to a tree with NO ROPE

IMPRESSIVENESS: ★ ★ ★ ★ ☆

CLASS: TWEENER/PRANK

FACTORS: COOPERATIVE MARK, SURPRISING END

REQUIRES: COOPERATIVE MARK AND A TREE

This one's similar to the "stick your friends to the bar" prank, but *so* much more evil. Plus: you can do it outside, and all you'll need is a tree.

Promise your friend he's about to try something cool, but don't say what it is (for this to work, the victim will have to cooperate at first . . . and you don't want to telegraph that you plan to totally screw him over).

"They really will be stuck, and it's not going to feel good. And you've got to decide how long you're comfortable letting them sit there and squirm . . . "

AUDIO

bit.ly/ZK9rku

Start by having him grab the tree with both of his hands, lean back slightly, and place his feet well in front of it. He'll look like he's straddling the tree, or trying to ride it like a broomstick. Then have him tuck his left foot in the crook of his right knee. Finally, as he slides down the tree, tuck his right foot under his left butt cheek. At this point, both of his feet should be pinned under different sides of his butt. If a foot is halfway out, lift him up and tuck it in.

Also: While you can theoretically do this on a street sign, I've found that the poles are too thin and too smooth. Even if you get into the proper position, anyone with reasonable upper body strength can probably pull himself up eventually.

At this point, give one good push down on his shoulders, and he should end up totally stuck. His feet are pinned under his butt, so he can't use his legs to stand up, and he won't have the leverage to pull his body up along the tree trunk. Plus, with his legs wrapped around the tree, the friction of the bark makes it even harder to move anything.

Remember that after 20-30 seconds, this will start hurting. Sitting in that awkward spot, unable to move is exceptionally tough . . . so try not to be too much of an evil jerk.

Big thanks to Dave Spencer for sending us this idea . . . we're still looking for an episode to put it in! (Strangely, there're not many trees around the bars we frequent . . .)

DEMONSTRATION

bit.ly/13sjbCY

THE SPELLiNG bee

IMPRESSiVENESS:
★ ★ ★ ☆ ☆

CLASS: TWEENER

FACTORS: THE TRICK FOOLS YOURSELF

REQUIRES: DECK OF CARDS

Grab a deck of cards right now, and we'll see if this works:

Start with any nine cards from the deck and place them face down into three piles of three cards each. Pick up any pile and look at the bottom card: that's your card, so remember it.

Place the pile you selected on top of either of the other two piles, then drop that combined pile onto the last one. Now things get interesting:

EPISODE

"The Spelling Bee is one of those very rare tricks that will actually fool yourself."

bit.ly/Y1zCrI

For each letter of the value of the card, deal one card face down onto the table as you spell it out. In other words, if your card is king, you would deal down four cards as you spelled "K-I-N-G." When finished, drop the rest of the cards on the pile you just dealt.

Next, spell "O-F" as you deal two more cards to the table. Drop the remaining cards on top.

Then spell the suit of the card as you deal down one card for each letter. Remember, suits are plural, so for clubs, you would deal five cards, spelling "C-L-U-B-S." Again, drop the remaining cards on top.

bit.ly/17NoFsL

AUDIO

Finally, pick any five letter word and spell it out as you deal. It could be "S-C-A-M-S," or "M-A-G-I-C," or even your own name (as long as it's five letters long).

Ready for the reveal? Turn over the last card you dealt . . . if you followed the instructions carefully, it should be your original card.

As we explain in the episode, this works on a couple of simple mathematical principles, and will work for any card in the entire deck. No matter what cards are selected, no matter how much they're shuffled, no matter which deck you pick . . . as long as you follow the steps correctly, it'll work.

DEMONSTRATION

bit.ly/ZGi2YF

SCIENCE FRICTION

IMPRESSIVENESS:
★ ★ ★ ★ ☆

CLASS: TWEENER

FACTORS: TABLE TRICK, FUN TO TEACH

REQUIRES: SALT SHAKER, STRAW WITH PAPER WRAPPER

Make everyone believes you can move an object *with your freakin' mind.*

The Effect: A straw is placed on a salt shaker, and moved with your mind.

The Method: No, you don't blow on it, and neither does anyone else.

You use static electricity and a diabolically clever way to charge the straw: simply pinch down tightly on the straw wrapper as you slide it off of the straw . . . there's no need to rub the straw on anything.

EPISODE

AUDIO

bit.ly/13VdxOg

bit.ly/11hhPt3

bit.ly/YKxoYI

Remember when performing this: *less is more.* If you just move the straw once or twice, you'll have a miracle. Any more than that, and they'll know exactly what you're up to.

. . . Unless you feel like teaching them, in which case get everyone at the table doing it. That's fun, too.

DEMONSTRATION

This mere action will (1) flatten the straw so it balances easier on the salt shaker, and (2) sufficiently charge the straw to spin as you move your hands around it.

As you play with this effect, remember that everyone's going to think you're blowing on it, so make sure to cancel out that possibility by having them hold a hand in front of your mouth. To get an effect from a farther distance, try holding your fists on opposite sides on opposite ends of the straw (upper right and

lower left corners, for example). This way you'll double the amount of force twisting the straw, and get a farther range.

For an even *more* remote movement, charge a second straw just like you did the first, and point it at the first straw. The straws are repulsive to each other, and on a dry day you'll get movement from a shockingly far distance. Plus, it will feel like you're casting some kind of fast food spell.

I want to give a huge thanks to magician Mike Powers for allowing us to teach his subtleties for this trick on Scam School. It's been one of my favorite impromptu effects for years, and I'm glad we got to share it.

DEMONSTRATION

bit.ly/12FaXsh

Cheat & Win at a
DrinkingRace

IMPRESSIVENESS:

★ ★ ★ ★ ☆

CLASS: TWEENER

FACTORS: BIG SETUP, FUN PAYOFF

REQUIRES: TALL BENDY STRAWS, PINT GLASSES, BOTTLES OF BEER

Next, you're going to challenge your friends to a drinking race that you're guaranteed to win . . . It's all about *physics*, man.

The Setup: Grab a couple of bottles of beer (or soda) and a bendy straw that's at least as tall as your bottle. Place pint glasses next to them and set up the following challenge:

The Challenge: Without moving the bottles (imagine they're glued to the table), be the first to get all the beer from your bottle into the pint glass.

Oh, and all the liquid **must** pass through the straw.

EPISODE

bit.ly/jf7eeW

As soon as you say go, most people will start slurping up mouthfuls of beer and spitting them into the pint glass. Others will do that thing where you place their finger over the top to trap the liquid one straw-full at a time. But you, on the other hand . . .

The Solution: Give them as much of a head start as you'd like, then bend the top of your straw over and aim for the pint glass. Seal your mouth over the bottle and the straw, then blow. The internal increase in pressure will shoot the beer out of the straw and into the pint glass.

DEMONSTRATION

AUDIO

bit.ly/YKy5RT

bit.ly/1OwpSHo

When done correctly, it'll look like you've turned your bottle into a keg tap, and all of the liquid will shoot through in less than 20 seconds.

Hypothetically, I suppose you could use this same technique in a real drinking race. Not that I recommend it, but if you were to race your friends to see who can down a (root?) beer the fastest, you can get an unfair advantage by placing bendy-straw in your bottle as you drink. The straw will allow air inside as you drink, eliminating the need to pause and let air bubble back into the bottle.

Then you'd be able to drink the whole tasty beverage in one fast motion, much faster than your friends.

... *Hypothetically.*

Remember that it is important that your straw reach all the way to the bottom of the bottle. Otherwise, you're only going to get down to the bottom quarter or so of the drink and feel like a chump.

Pool Hall Scams

IMPRESSIVENESS:

★★★★☆ – ★★★★★

CLASS: CLOSER

FACTORS: WIDE VARIETY, VARYING UTILITY

REQUIRES: A POOL TABLE

EPISODE 1

bit.ly/ZGiIgD

I'll be honest, I'm not the best pool player. Hell, I'm not even what most would call "acceptable." But I have learned a couple of cool tricks and sucker bets to use at the pool table.

You've Got Nothing!

While halfway through playing a standard game of 8 ball, start calling out your opponent. Tell him he stinks. Tell him he's got nothin'. In fact, claim that you're so much better than him, *he won't sink another ball for the rest of the entire game.*

Once he accepts your bet, take your turn . . . and immediately sink the 8-ball. You'll lose the game, but you'll win the side bet.

bit.ly/bAkriX

EPISODE 2

bit.ly/12azq7M

Spot-On

AUDIO

THE SETUP: Place a ball on the table's spot (or set on top of any bill), then place a dime on top of the ball. Fire the cue ball forward, knock the ball off, and watch as the dime lands right on the spot (or in the circle frame of the bill's portrait).

After showing you can pull it off every time, challenge them to get it right just 2 out of 3 times. They won't have a chance.

THE REVEAL: When you set the dime up for yourself, place it squarely on the center-top of the ball. When you set it up for them, tilt it slightly to the back of the ball. This way, when the ball is struck, the dime will be launched backwards and away from the target spot.

Clean Slate

Start playing a simple game of 8-ball with your friends . . . about halfway through the game, offer an alternative face-off: if your friend can clear every ball off the table without scratching once, you'll buy him a beer. He gets unlimited turns, and doesn't have to sink a ball each time, but if he scratches, he owes you a beer.

Fair enough?

Let him play through the whole table, eventually getting down to just the cue ball . . . at which point you remind him of your bargain: if your friend can clear *every ball* off the table

without scratching once, you'll buy him a beer . . . and there's no way to clear off the *cue ball* without scratching.

Side Bet

Set up one ball (we'll say the six) on the bumper of the table, supported by two other balls (if the bumper edge of your table is too steep, just keep adding balls in line as you see in this photo).

Bet your friend he can't hit the six without touching the other two balls . . . after several attempts, tell him you can do it.

When it's your turn, gently hit the six forward, and during its slow journey across the table, use your hip to bump the table. This will jostle the balls just enough to drop the six-ball down off the bumper, so it's the only one hit.

In a Pinch

Start playing a super-simple nonsense game on the pool table: each of you put a ball next to the bumper and use a single index finger to pinch downward on the back-top of the ball. After enough pressure, the ball will "squirt" out and forward. After a few practice rounds, each of you should have a feel for how it works. Now, challenge him to a face off for a beer: whoever gets their ball to roll the farthest wins. In fact, each of you can have 3 attempts to make it more fair.

For the first couple of attempts, do the squeeze move exactly as he does. But on the third attempt, lick your index finger. This time, instead of the downward pressure creating backspin, your slick finger will slide effortlessly down the back of the ball, launching it with nothing but forward momentum. It'll make it all the way across the table, and you'll win the game.

sweet VICTORY

This one is based on an old gambling scam. It's a simple impromptu game you can play while you wait for your meal . . . Oh, and it's totally rigged.

The Setup: Grab a fistful of sugar packets and start writing the numbers 1–9 on them. Lay them in a pile and announce that you're about to have a tournament of sugar packets, so everyone must pick their winner and write it down.

EPISODE

bit.ly/bW8SkB

AUDIO

bit.ly/1OwqrBb

The tournament is played out by shuffling the packets and tossing them in the air. Once they land, any face-down packet is eliminated, while the ones with numbers showing stay in the game. Keep playing until only one numbered packet remains . . . unsurprisingly, the number matches your prediction.

The Work: Before starting the game, secretly make sure you've already written the number "4" on the back of the fourth packet down.

When you write the numbers 1–9 on the packets, you'll have secretly created a "double-headed" sugar packet, guaranteeing you the win.

playing THE ODDS

EPISODE

bit.ly/ZlKKPH

If you're comfortable with taking a little risk for a chance at a HUGE reward, you will love these two impossibilities that rely on people's inherent misunderstanding of probability.

5-Card Mind Control: Let's try a little mental experiment, just me and you. I've picked out five cards from the deck. Take a quick look at them, because in a moment I'm going to ask you to choose one. Before you do though, keep in mind that I might be trying to manipulate you into picking an obvious card, so think hard, take a moment, and choose one of the five cards on the top of next page.

AUDIO

bit.ly/13ski5M

Most people choose the seven of clubs or the four of hearts . . . But I'm going to guess you picked . . . *the four of hearts*. Was I right?

This is an old classic called Dai Vernon's 5-card force. And it's super easy to do.

In front of your friend, lay down (in this order) the king of hearts, the seven of clubs, the ace of diamonds, the four of hearts, and the nine of diamonds. Ask her to mentally choose any card. The key to this one is dropping just a hint that you might try to influence their decision. Once you mention that, they'll eliminate the ace of diamonds as too obvious. They'll eliminate the seven of clubs since it's the only black card. They'll eliminate the king of hearts as the only face card, and (for some reason), nobody seems to like the nine of diamonds.

In my personal experience, if they don't pick the four of hearts, it's usually the seven of clubs. So in performance, I'll have them select a card, then I'll scoop them all up and mix them around. Finally, I'll pull out the seven of clubs and hold it face down in my hand as I ask "Were you thinking of the four of hearts?" If I'm right, the trick is over.

But if I'm wrong, I'll ask "Hm . . . if you don't mind telling me: what was your card?" If she says the seven of clubs, I'll smile and turn over my "**real**" guess: the seven of clubs.

If, just now, you didn't pick the four of hearts, don't hold it against the trick. Obviously, it's way different trying to perform a magic trick through text. Just try it as a throwaway trick a few times with your friends and see how well it's received.

Side-by-Side: Next, a twist of probability that blew my mind when I first experienced it: grab a deck of cards and shuffle them. I'm serious . . . I want you to try this.

Now think of any two random card values (from ace through king, and don't worry about suits). In your mind, what would you guess the odds are that two cards of *exactly those values* are right next to each other in your deck?

Are the odds 20%?

...10%?

...1%?

If we were sitting at the bar right now, would you bet a beer that those two numbers are more likely to be *together* or *apart* in the deck?

Amazingly (and to just about everyone's disbelief), it seems that about 50% of the time, any two named values will just happen to be side-by-side in a shuffled deck of cards.

I now *know* that the odds are just a hair under 50%, because mathematician James Grime of Cambridge University just so happened to be a fan of scam school. And when he saw me incorrectly guess that the odds were 70% (which I assumed based on my handful of trials), he put together an awesome YouTube video calling me out and giving the correct statistics.

SPECIAL RESPONSE
FROM JAMES GRIME

bit.ly/45d941

bRAIN dRAIN

The problem with most ESP/ mind-reading effects is that they're just so damned *boring*. There's no real interaction or personality to them. That's what's great about the Brain Drain. It's so dead simple you can do it with any of your friends, and so over the top that everyone can't help but have a good time watching it.

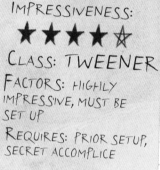

IMPRESSIVENESS:
★ ★ ★ ★ ☆

CLASS: TWEENER

FACTORS: HIGHLY IMPRESSIVE, MUST BE SET UP

REQUIRES: PRIOR SETUP, SECRET ACCOMPLICE

The Setup: Five objects are laid out in front of the scammer, and while the scammer's eyes are covered, one is selected by the group (or has an object hidden within it). The would-be psychic individually grabs the faces of each of his spectators (like some kind of idiotic mind-meld) and attempts to read their minds to know which object is the selected one . . .

And amazingly, he figures it out every time.

EPISODE

bit.ly/b08j5i

bit.ly/YKyOSU

AUDIO

The Secret: No surprise here, but ESP has nothing to do with it. Instead, pre-arrange for one of the spectators to be your secret assistant, and work out a simple number code for each of the objects on the table. When we did this on Scam School we simply numbered the containers 1 through 5.

The method of communication between you and your secret assistant is diabolical: Make a big show as you put your hands on each person's face, but when you get to your secret assistant, make sure your fingers cover both of his temples. As soon as you grab him, your assistant will clench his teeth in a number of pulses, corresponding to the secret number you're looking for.

Nobody will see the motion, but you'll clearly feel the pulses on your fingertips . . . Try it on your temples right now: put your fingers on your temples and clench down on your teeth a few times.

Once you have the secret number, you're good to go, and to everyone else it will look like you're a damned wizard!

HOW TO MAKE A
MARKED
DECK

IMPRESSIVENESS:

★ ★ ★ ★ ★

CLASS: GIMMICK

FACTORS: MAJOR PRE-WORK, PRACTICE REQUIRED

REQUIRES: SHARPIE MARKER, DECK OF BICYCLE CARDS

EPISODE

bit.ly/ZGj9aC

There's a million ways to make a marked deck of cards, but here's a quick and easy method that we taught on Scam School: you'll need a red-backed deck of rider-back Bicycle cards, a red sharpie marker, and about 30 minutes of your time.

This is going to be tedious, but *oh, man* will it be worth it . . . You'll have an advantage in every game of cards you ever play again. If a card trick goes awry, you'll always be able to save it by knowing what card they took. This is the swiss-army knife of card gimmicks.

If you ever suspect you're playing with a marked deck, there's an easy way to check: square up all the cards and riffle through them as if they're a flip book. In a marked deck, you'll see a wild scattershot of tiny imperfections and markings jumping all over the back of the cards.

AUDIO

bit.ly/1Ob5vIp

Can you figure out what card this is?

I've heard this called "going to the movies" by gamblers.

Take a look at the upper right hand corner of the back design.

We're going to encode the value of the card into the small pinwheel, and we'll encode the suit into the ocean-wave-looking dots just below and to the right.

With your red sharpie marker, you'll find that a single dot over any one of those petals makes them totally vanish, and it's surprisingly hard to notice. As you go through the deck, also remember that you'll need to mark both ends of each card. Each time you finish one corner, rotate the card 180 degrees and start again, making the same marks on the other side.

number/face

Suit

DEMONSTRATION

bit.ly/Y1AyfN

Let's start with the pinwheel: if the card is an **ace**, we'll leave the pinwheel totally unmarked.

For the numbers **2 through 10**, we'll place marks moving clockwise around the pinwheel, starting with 2 at the top and ending with the center dot being 10.

Finally, for the **jack**, **queen**, **and king**, we'll place two marks: marking both the center dot and top petal will be "jack," marking both the center and the second petal will be "queen," and marking both the center and the third petal is "king."

Now the ocean wave: the first four triangles are going to be our code for the suit. You can pick any order for the suits, but I like arranging them as "**clubs**," "**hearts**," "**spades**," and "**diamonds**." This is an easy one to remember because they're in CHSD, or "CHaSeD" order, as magicians call it.

. . . oh and by the way, did you end up figuring out the example card at the beginning of the chapter? (If you picked the 10 of diamonds, a winner is you!)

If you're worried about remembering this code, don't be. The good news is that the very act of spending 30 minutes making this deck means that by the time you're done, you've practiced enough that the translation will be totally automatic. Keep in mind also that there's a good chance you'll mess up at least one card as you mark them, so have a second deck handy. When you mess up, just swap out your bad card for a clean one.

MENTAL MASTERY

IMPRESSIVENESS:
★ ★ ★ ★ ★

CLASS: TWEENER

FACTORS: MASSIVE UTILITY, HIGHLY VERSATILE

REQUIRES: STUFF TO WRITE ON, PRESENTATION SKILLS

EPISODE

bit.ly/11JgWZo

This is one of the most powerful principles you'll learn in this book. I've put together a super-simple version of the trick that you'll be able to perform at the bar with virtually no preparation, but there are much more advanced versions that use the exact same technique and will blow you away.

AUDIO

bit.ly/XTFIbm

The Effect: After the scammer jots down a guess and hides it in a glass, three volunteers are each individually asked completely fair, random questions . . . anything from the name of their first pet to a random color they're thinking of. Yet, after everyone has "locked in" their answers, our fake psychic shows that he guessed all *three of their answers in advance!*

The Method: It doesn't matter what the questions you ask are. In fact, the more creative and strange the questions you ask, the more fun this will be for everyone. "How tall was your dad?" "What year were you born?" "What's the name of the first person you ever kissed?"

All you need to pull this one off is the ability to force just *one* of the three answers in advance. You can pre-arrange an answer with one of your friends, you can force a particular playing card, or ask a question that you already know the answer to. Heck, you could even just guess at a yes-or-no question. Even if you get that one question wrong, you'll still be right for 2 out of 3.

This effect relies on the fake psychic working out-of-order.

After asking the first question, you'll think, focus, and secretly write the answer to the *third* question you plan to ask (this is the one "force" question that you already know the answer to). Fold up the paper and place it in the glass.

their answers	you write
1. apple	1. 2 of clubs
2. New York	2. apple
3. Science	3. New York
4. 2 of clubs	4. Science

↑ forced answer

"Now I don't want to accuse you of being this kind of person," you say, "but some people like to mess with me and they'll lie after the trick is over and say I got it wrong. Since I've already locked in my first guess, let everyone else know what you were thinking of."

She'll announce her first answer, and you'll now know your *second* prediction to write.

Continue to write down the answer to each previous question until you finally get to the one question you've pre-arranged the answer to. This will be your last prediction.

Finally, shake up the predictions inside the glass as you ask everyone to reiterate their previous answers, and for the reveal, pour out the jumbled guesses and hand each one to its correct match.

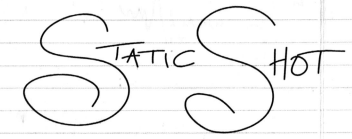

STATIC SHOT

AUDIO

bit.ly/Y1AI6N

IMPRESSIVENESS:
★ ★ ★ ★ ★

CLASS: TWEENER

FACTORS: ACTING SKILL, PRACTICE

REQUIRES: SUGAR PACKETS

This effect has everything: it's fun to do, it looks impressive, it makes you feel like you've got superpowers, and most importantly . . . it lets you make someone else look like an idiot.

The Scam: Tear off the edges of a sweetener packet and dump out the contents. This should leave you with a sheet of thin paper with a crease down the middle. This will be your "target." Set up your target a foot or so away from your outstretched arm, making sure to keep it as precariously balanced as you're able (the easier it is to knock over, the better it works).

bit.ly/15E52GZ

EPISODE

bit.ly/17NrwSn

Next, put on a show of slapping your face and rubbing your cheeks to "build up a static charge," and finally, after rubbing your **left cheek** with your **right hand**, keep your hand wide and flat as you swing it in a wide arc from your face, eventually ending up pointing at the target.

Pause for just a second or two, make a finger gun, and pull the trigger. As if shot, the packet will fall over.

If you do the move correctly, as you swing your hand out, you will generate a gust of air that will take a couple of seconds to reach the target. Once you have your timing down, it will appear that you simply point and

"fire" your finger gun to knock over the target.

It'll take some practice to get it down, but once you've got it, it's a blast. Be warned though: your friends will be suspicious. First they'll think you're just blowing to knock it over, so let them keep a hand in front of your face as you perform it. In fact, you can bit.ly/10wrm4o

prove that there's *no way* wind can be involved by placing a bottle or pint glass between you and the paper. Unbelievably, that gust of wind you generate will roll right around the glass and *still* knock over the paper.

Here's the Best Part: your friends will want to know how it's done. Explain that it's all about the static electricity generated by rubbing and slapping their face. Demonstrate the moves for them, really rubbing and slapping your face. But when you demonstrate the moves for them, move your **right hand** from your **right cheek**.

When you do the moves this way, you don't generate that gust of wind, *but they won't notice the difference in moves*. They'll think they're doing the exact same thing, but for some reason it just won't work for them. The harder they try, the funnier it gets.

The first time I saw this performed was by Daniel Garcia, and it utterly floored me. I later found out it's published in the works of our Scam School friend Diamond Jim Tyler. Thanks again to both of them for making me feel dumb.

10 CARD Poker Scam

AUDIO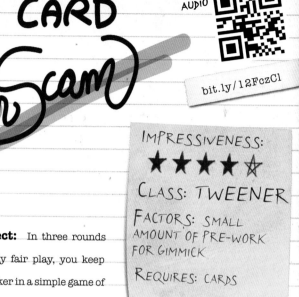

bit.ly/12FczCl

IMPRESSIVENESS:
★ ★ ★ ★ ☆

CLASS: TWEENER

FACTORS: SMALL AMOUNT OF PRE-WORK FOR GIMMICK

REQUIRES: CARDS

The Effect: In three rounds of increasingly fair play, you keep beating the sucker in a simple game of poker.

The Setup: Start by grabbing 3 sets of 3 cards (in our example, we used 3 jacks, 3 queens, and 3 eights). Then add one singular card to act as the "poison" card. It should be a high value card that would normally be desirable in a game of poker (we used the king of clubs).

Last, mark the back of the "poison" card in a subtle way that only you will see (we used a red felt-tip pen to color in a dot on the back of the card, similar to how we made our marked deck a few chapters ago).

EPISODE

bit.ly/12aBNaK

The Secret: Each time you deal the cards, whoever gets the poison card will lose. Now, you'll never know in advance what the hands will be (could be a three-of-a-kind beating a two pair, or a full house beating a three-of-a-kind), but just remember that *whoever gets the poison card loses*.

PHASE #1: Mix up the cards, and make sure to keep the poison card at the bottom. Deal out two hands of cards such that the last card is given to your sucker. Compare hands and show you win.

PHASE #2: Suggest that it might be more fair if you let him pick some of his own cards. Mix up the cards again, and this time, make sure the poison card is on top. Start showing him cards, one at a time, and have him decide either to keep the card for himself, or to give it to you.

Make sure he sees the poison card first, and because it's such a high card, he'll want it for himself.

Run through a few more cards, then once you've made it through half the deck, have him choose the remainder of cards face down. Again, compare hands, and you'll see that you win.

PHASE #3: Explain that the fairest way of all to pick cards would be simply to mix them all up face down and have take turns pulling out your cards from the pile. Make sure you go first, and simply avoid taking the marked poison card. Once he has it, *he's screwed*.

fine dining

IMPRESSIVENESS:

★ ★ ★ ★ ☆

CLASS: CLOSER

FACTORS: NOVEL PUZZLE, SURPRISING ANSWER

REQUIRES: FANCY RESTAURANT WITH TABLECLOTHS

We do a variety of puzzles on Scam School, but never one with such an unfair setup, or such a surprising solution . . .

The Setup: In any restaurant with a tablecloth, place a dime between two nickels and then balance an upside-down glass on the two nickels. For the best effect, have a lot of other stuff around: knives, forks, napkins, sugar packets, straws . . . the more odds and ends, the better.

The Challenge: Get the dime out from its prison without touching the glass or the coins, *and* without touching anything with another object.

EPISODE

bit.ly/15EVivZ

I've noticed that this works best when the tablecloth is a bit loose, and it definitely doesn't work at all if you have no finger-nails.

So no pushing the glass with a straw, and (spoiler alert!) you won't be able to slide a knife under the glass without accidentally touching it. Some people will try to use a straw to blow the coin out, to no avail. Others will shake the table, but once the glass falls off of the nickels, the dime becomes completely trapped.

I like to add an extra red herring by reminding them they can use "*anything on the table*" to make it work. That way, they'll spend more time focusing on random objects and less time thinking outside the box.

DEMONSTRATION

bit.ly/15EVxH1

The Payoff: Using your fingernail, scratch at the cloth in front of the coin, and the dime will slowly "walk" its way out of the glass.

No, really: I'm serious. And it looks awesome, to boot.

Pool Shark

IMPRESSIVENESS:
★ ★ ★ ☆ ☆

CLASS: CLOSER

FACTORS: WIDE VARIETY, VARYING UTILITY

REQUIRES: A POOL TABLE

Half the fun of this scam is watching your suckers try to pull it off. Because the obvious technique involves jumping the cue over another ball, expect to see a *lot* of balls flying off the table. And because each time they'll be convinced that they *almost got it that time* . . . expect them to stubbornly continue to attempt it.

The Hook: Line up three pool balls directly in front of a side pocket. About 6 inches back, place the 8-ball. Finally set up the cue ball behind the 8-ball and make the following claim: With only a single strike of the cue ball, you'll be able to sink **all three** pool balls right into that side pocket, **without** anything touching the 8-ball.

Now let them go for it. With each attempt, insist that they *almost had it that time.* They'll try jumping over the 8-ball, banking off the side rails, and occasionally, actually get close to pulling it off . . .

bit.ly/15FTkvn

EPISODE

AUDIO

bit.ly/11yKzzg

. . . but once they confess they can't do it, prove them wrong.

The Sinker: Place the triangle around the 8-ball, lining one corner up with the first of the three balls in a row. Now with just a simple tap, the cue ball hits the triangle, the triangle sinks the three balls . . . all without anything touching the 8-ball.

NAPKIN chess

IMPRESSIVENESS:
★ ★ ★ ☆ ☆

CLASS: CLOSER

FACTORS: LENGTHY GAME, CAREFUL EXECUTION REQUIRED

REQUIRES: NAPKIN, A WHOLE LOT OF LOOSE CHANGE

It seems like everyone makes up goofy little games to pass the time at the bar — here's one with a secret method that will guarantee you the win:

The Setup: Lay out a small cocktail napkin and bunch of pocket change (and I mean a **lot** of it . . . quarters, dimes, nickels, etc.).

EPISODE

bit.ly/aaTnEn

AUDIO

bit.ly/ZlMOaC

The Rules: Take turns placing coins on the napkin. You can lay down any size coin you want, anywhere on the napkin, just as long as nothing goes over the edge or touches another coin. The *loser* is the one who on his turn can't find a proper place to set their coin on the napkin without violating the rules. (Oh, and no balancing coins on their edges).

BUT WAIT!

The Scam: Play a few games. Win some. Lose some. Once you're playing for money (or beer), move in for the kill: go first and place one coin in the exact center of the napkin. After that, place your coins in an *exact* mirror image of your opponents' moves. As long as you copy their every move, there's no possible outcome except for the napkin filling up perfectly on your turn.

Special thanks go to the fantastic Todd Robbins for giving us permission to cover this gem. His book *Modern Con Man* would be a fantastic addition to any scammer's library.

Behold the wonder!

bit.ly/10b6iZW

EPISODE

bit.ly/Y1BaC5

AUDIO

light a MATCH with your TEETH

IMPRESSIVENESS:
★★★★☆

CLASS: OPENER

FACTORS: DANGEROUS, HAZARDOUS

REQUIRES: BOX OF STRIKE-ANYWHERE MATCHES

Look like a complete badass by lighting a match with your teeth!

WARNING: Okay, so we're playing with matches here. I shouldn't have to tell you that only responsible adults should attempt any of these feats, and under proper safety conditions. I should also point out that if you attempt ANY of these tricks, you absolutely **WILL GET BURNED**.

Also: please don't burn anything down. And don't sue me.

There. Warnings are out of the way. Yes you'll get burned, but man, you'll look so badass.

Do you have what it takes to light a match with your teeth?

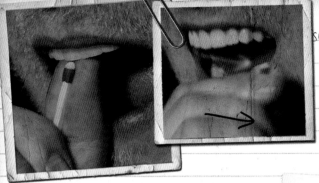

DEMONSTRATION

bit.ly/ZlNahx

Grab a box of "strike anywhere" matches, and pick out the ones that have the most of that white strikey-anywherey stuff on them (That's the scientific term, right?). They absolutely must be strike-anywhere matches, which are apparently harder to find in some areas.

Before you begin, dry off your teeth. When you're first practicing, use a paper towel to make sure they're completely dry. Later (as you get more practiced), you'll be able to just use your fingers to dry your teeth out enough.

Now, what happens next is going to depend on the shape of your teeth, so you're going to have to experiment with a few different variations on these moves:

Place the match in the part of your teeth that will have the maximum strike area. For a lucky few, it'll be the crook in-between their front two incisors. If you're one of those people, you'll be able place your thumb behind the match inside your mouth and pop the match straight forward, and just that small amount of friction will light it.

Remember that your goal is to have enough friction to cause enough heat to get the match started, so you'll have to put a decent amount of pressure against your teeth as you push forward.

If you try it a few times but get nothing, try this sure-fire variation: hold the match pointing straight upward, with the head touching the bottom-right-hand edge of your right incisor. I want you to pretend that the bottoms of your two incisors is your striking surface, and your goal is to drag the

Oh, and NEWS FLASH: I have no idea what this does to your teeth in the long term . . . but I can't imagine it's good.

match head along it all the way from the beginning of the right edge to the end of the left edge.

You'll need a tight grip right underneath the match head to keep it in position, and you'll have to keep it firmly placed against the bottom of your teeth as you drag it across. If your match keeps falling off the "strike surface" of your teeth as you drag across, try pinching your fingers actually *on* each side of the match head, and use the tips of your fingers to keep everything lined up. This is super effective, but increases the risk of burning the tips of your

fingers . . .
(I did mention
that you'll totally
get burned doing
this eventually,
right?)

easy
BOOK
test

bit.ly/ZitzOK

EPISODE

IMPRESSIVENESS:
★ ★ ★ ☆ ☆

CLASS: TWEENER

FACTORS: PRACTICE, ABILITY TO KEEP PROCESS INTERESTING

REQUIRES: 1 TO 3 BOOKS OR MAGAZINES

The "book test" plot is a standard in stage mentalist performances: a random volunteer picks a random book, a random page, and then a random word . . . and yet the wizard somehow knows the secretly thought-of word. Hell, I do a version of it in my stage show, and it's one of my favorite effects.

It took me *years* to perfect the method I use, but you'll be performing this version in minutes . . . and for just about everyone, the effect will look exactly the same as what I do on stage. You'll get all the credit, and put in none of the work . . . you damned dirty *cheater*!

The Effect: A randomly selected word is chosen from a randomly selected book . . . yet without peeking or cheating, you tell them which word they're thinking of.

AUDIO

bit.ly/ZitCcI

The Method: The first thing you'll have her do is pick a book: When we taught this on Scam School, I offered 3 choices, but it works just as well with only one book.

Next, have her pick a 3 digit number, with 3 different digits (for example, she can't choose something like 777, 224, or 838). This number will be truly random, but by having her make a couple of calculations, you'll be able to force a particular outcome with the following steps:

1. To make the chosen number "even more random," reverse all 3 digits, and **subtract** the smaller number from the larger. (In other words, if your first number was 123, you would subtract that from 321, giving you 198.)

2. Take your *new* number, reverse the digits again, and this time **add** the two together. (In our example, we would add 198 to 891, giving us 1089.)

example

$$\begin{array}{r} 894 \\ -\ 498 \\ \hline 396 \end{array}$$

step 1.

$$\begin{array}{r} 396 \\ +\ 693 \\ \hline 1089 \end{array}$$

step 2.

Here's the Scam:

every time you follow these steps, you will always get 1089. (Try it a few times; I know you don't believe me.)

By this point, your target believes she's ended up with a 100% completely random number. After all, she picked the original 3 digit number, and all this math mumbo-jumbo could only make it even *more* random, right?

Acting as if you have no idea what her number is, tell them the last digit will be the "word number," and all the digits before it will be the "page number."

Of course, every time you do this trick, it'll be page 108, word number 9, but it's important that you act like you didn't know that. Have them open the book, find the word (which you've of course memorized in advance), then reveal that you've *actually read her mind.*

Next, take her newfound trust and use it to start a cult. (You'll have to buy a bunch of white robes for this part). Move to the Nevada desert and build a compound where tacos are illegal and nobody is allowed to use the letter Q.

(This last part is just an optional kicker ending to the routine.)

IMPRESSIVENESS:
★★★☆☆

CLASS: TWEENER

FACTORS: REQUIRES PRACTICE

REQUIRES: 3 RANDOM OBJECTS, COLLECTION OF SMALL COUNTERS

From the genius mind of Martin Gardner, "Gardner's purloined objects" is a fun logic trick that will allow you to deduce which of your friends has a stolen object in their pocket. This may look a bit overwhelming as you read it, but I promise it's not nearly as hard as it sounds . . . plus, it's way fun to pull off.

The Setup: Grab 3 random friends and 3 random objects (we'll refer to these random objects as A, B, and C here). Dump out a container of exactly 24 Tic Tacs, matches, or coins (it's important that you have exactly 24 counters, but it's equally important that you *act* like you don't even know or care how many there are).

Next, pass out a few of the Tic Tacs so one of your players has 1, another has 2, and the last has 3. From this point forward, think of your "suspects" as #1, #2, and #3, and your "stolen objects" as letters A, B, and C.

EPISODE

bit.ly/r6GsfE

AUDIO

bit.ly/YKAOe9

How to view the table

Turn your back and ask each of your players to "steal" one object and hide it somewhere you won't find it.

The Game: Now by giving a few instructions (without looking), you'll be able to figure out who took which object. While looking away (or blindfolded) give the following instructions to your suspects:

"Whoever took object A: I want you think of how many Tic Tacs you were given . . . Now take that number out of the pile and eat them."

"Whoever took object B: I want you think of how many Tic Tacs you were given . . . Now take **TWICE** that number out of the pile and eat them."

"Whoever took object C: I want you think of how many Tic Tacs you were given. Now take **FOUR TIMES** number out of the pile and eat them."

When you turn around, there will be some number of Tic Tacs left over (between 1 and 7 of them). *This number will reveal to you who has which object*, but of course you can't act like you even care what that number is. Instead, just say "Oh, cool — there's some left for me!" and eat them all.

Remember, each person has a number of Tic Tacs assigned to them, and each stolen object has a letter assigned to it. So here's how the number of leftover Tic Tacs gives you the answer of who took what:

- 1 Tic Tac: Person 1 has A, 2 has B, 3 has C
- 2 Tic Tacs: Person 1 has B, 2 has A, 3 has C
- 3 Tic Tacs: Person 1 has A, 2 has C, 3 has B
- 4 Tic Tacs: Not possible
- 5 Tic Tacs: Person 1 has B, 2 has C, 3 has A
- 6 Tic Tacs: Person 1 has C, 2 has A, 3 has B
- 7 Tic Tacs: Person 1 has C, 2 has B, 3 has A

. . . now that's a lot to keep track of, but luckily, there's one magic sentence that will make it SUPER easy to remember:

ABsolutely, BriAn's ACtive shows

Person 1 *Person 2* *Person 1* *Person 2* *you messed up!*

1 tic tac 2 tic tacs 3 4

BeCkon CheAting ContriButions

5 6 7

"**AB**solutely, **B**ri**A**n's **AC**tive shows **B**e**C**kon **C**he**A**ting **C**ontri**B**utions."

It's a silly sentence, but as long as you remember it, you'll know who has which object. Each word corresponds to a number (1–7), and the capitalized letters tell you, in order, what object person 1 and person 2 have. So if you turn around and there are 3 Tic Tacs left, you'll look at the third word, "ACtive," and know that person one has object A, person 2 has C, and (by default,) person 3 has B.

If you turn around and there's only 1 Tic Tac, then you think of "**AB**solutely," and you'll know that person 1 has object A, person 2 has object B, and (by default,) person 3 must have object C.

To make this as easy as possible on yourself, make sure to choose 3 objects that are easy to associate with the letters A, B, and C.

Oh, and that magic sentence mnemonic? That came (along with the suggestion for the episode) from Scott Cram, who has sent in several ideas that have turned into some of my favorite episodes of Scam School. Scott runs the Grey Matters blog, a fantastic site dedicated to awesome quirky mathematical and logic puzzles.

Psychic MATCHBOOKS

IMPRESSIVENESS:
★★★☆☆

CLASS: TWEENER

FACTORS: COMPLETELY IMPROMTU, SURPRISINGLY POWERFUL

REQUIRES: 3 MATCHBOOKS

This is just about the simplest, most impromptu mind-reading effect I know. You just need 3 simple matchbooks for a mental miracle to earn yourself an easy free drink. I'll be giving you the basic mechanics of the trick here, but it's up to you to add character and story to the presentation. Of course, you can check out the Scam School episode to see the performance I threw together for this scam, but I encourage you to discover your own take on it.

EPISODE

bit.ly/bSAi3R

How It Looks: Three matchbooks are set in front of the mark. While you turn around (or even leave the room), he's invited to grab any matchbook and sneakily remove one match from anywhere, hide the match, and replace the matchbook in the exact same place.

Once you turn back around, you pick up each matchbook and weigh it in the palm of your hand. After holding up each one in turn, you boldly (and correctly) reveal which matchbook is missing a match.

How It's Done: I'm sure you can guess that the weight of the matchbooks has nothing to do with it. Before the trick begins, pretend to feel each matchbook for a "baseline" weight. As you fuss

bit.ly/YKAZGe

AUDIO

DEMONSTRATION

bit.ly/Y1Buk3

over each one, push each matchbook cover super-tightly into the flap
at the base. Once all three covers are firmly pushed in, you're set.

They've picked out a match and you've turned back around to
"weigh" them again, but this time, apply slight movement with your
thumb on the matchbook cover and you'll discover that two of them
are still firmly pressed in, but one will be loose from the sucker
opening it.

Remember that you'll need to be *subtle* about this . . . that's
why I like the idea of "weighing" the matchbooks. It's a sensible
reason to get your hands on them, and it provides good cover for
surreptitiously thumbing the covers.

Remember, any time you perform a trick that requires someone
to follow instructions while you're not looking, it's
important you make your instructions **dead simple, and totally
clear.** After all, if they pick up multiple matchbooks,
they'll almost certainly dislodge one of the covers, and
your trick will flop.

Birthday Scam

Quick: in your own mind, imagine you're at a party with 35 to 40 people. What do you think the odds are that two people will share the *exact same birthday*?

Remember, we're looking at about 40 people in the room, and there's 365 days in the year, so would the odds be . . .

(a) **0-25%**

(b) **25%-50%**

(c) **50%-75%**

(d) **75%-85%**

(e) **Over 85%**

IMPRESSIVENESS:

★ ★ ★ ★ ☆

CLASS: CLOSER

FACTORS: LARGE GROUPS, POSSIBLE GIANT PAYOFF

REQUIRES: LARGE GROUP OF PEOPLE

Make your guess right now. (I'm serious. I want you to try this.) I've asked this question at hundreds of lectures across colleges nationwide, and the vast majority of people tend to pick (a) or (b), with the occasional smartass going as high as (d) . . . but the shocking truth is that with 40 people in the room, the answer is (e), *there's over an 85% chance two people in the room have the same birthday.*

bit.ly/12FdFhx

EPISODE

AUDIO

bit.ly/13slG8w

This seems utterly insane to me! This is a case where the human mind just isn't wired correctly to grasp true probability. Most of us figure "okay, there's about 40 people and about 365 days . . . so the answer must be about 40/365 . . . which is about 10%." However, the true math is far more complex. There is a fancy Wikipedia article that goes into more detail about this.

Warning: if you visit that article you're going to see fancy math stuff like this:

. . . P(A') is equal to the product of these individual probabilities:

(1) $P(A') = 365/365 \times 364/365 \times 363/365 \times 362/365 \times \ldots \times 343/365$

The terms of equation (1) can be collected to arrive at:

(2) $P(A') = (1/365)23 \times (365 \times 364 \times 363 \times \ldots \times 343)$

Evaluating equation (2) gives $P(A') = 0.492703$

Therefore, $P(A) = 1 - 0.492703 = 0.507297$ (50.7297%) . . .

. . . but thankfully, you'll also see a super-simple graph showing the range of probabilities. And a few numbers to keep in mind when you're trying to decide if the time is right for you to play this trick.

(graphs and mumbers on the next page)

- The odds are **50%** you'll have a match with only **23** people in the room

- The odds are **80%** you'll have a match with only **35** people in the room

- The odds are **90%** you'll have a match with only **42** people in the room

- The odds are **99%** you'll have a match with only **57** people in the room (wow!)

With these numbers in mind, make sure to adjust your wager accordingly, but definitely remember that any time there are more than 23 people in the room, it's worth it for you to offer a simple even-money proposition.

STICK your friends to the BAR

IMPRESSIVENESS:
★ ★ ★ ★ ☆

CLASS: PRANK

FACTORS: JERK MOVE, ANGRY VICTIM

REQUIRES: A FULL PINT OF BEER, A BAR OR POOL TABLE

This clever trick uses a pint of beer and two willing thumbs to handcuff your friend (or enemy) to the bar, while you take his keys, wallet, girlfriend, and more.

The Prank: Have your friend order a pint of his favorite drink. The more expensive the drink, the better. Make sure the pint glass is filled all the way to the top. Ask your friend to put his thumbs on the edge of the bar (as pictured). Then, carefully set the full pint of drink on top of his thumbs. Tell him it's important to balance it perfectly.

EPISODE

bit.ly/ZitVV4

Now . . . get out of there! With his favorite drink precariously balanced on his thumbs, he has no possible way of chasing after you.

Eventually, he may figure out he can slurp some of the beer of the top, or bite the side of the glass . . . but by then you can be long gone.

AUDIO

bit.ly/12Fe6IC

DEMONSTRATION

bit.ly/15E6ERe

You could probably take his wallet, his keys, or whatever else you want, while you're at it.

Static Charge MATCH

IMPRESSIVENESS:
★ ★ ★ ★ ☆

CLASS: TWEENER

FACTORS: CONVINCING ILLUSION; PRESENTATION MATTERS

REQUIRES: WOODEN MATCHES, ACTING SKILLS, PRACTICE

I use this all the time. There's something so awesome about the buildup of anticipation, the fear of an explosion, and the utter surprise of a match launching two feet into the air that makes this one of the *best* bar tricks to pull.

The Effect: Start by having someone hold out her hand. Place a large wooden match on her palm, balanced halfway off. Now hold up another match in your hand. Start "building up static" by rubbing the match on your pants legs, shuffling your feet . . . doing anything that looks like you're about to give someone a shock.

Now slowly bring your "charged" match towards the one dangling off of her hand . . . and despite wood being an insulator, the moment the matches touch, her match will make an audible *crack* sound and soar up into the air!

EPISODE
bit.ly/ZMvI03

AUDIO

bit.ly/11hm0o0

The Method: Not to bum you out, but physics and static electricity have nothing to do with it. All you really need to do is use your fingernail to flick the base of your match right before both match heads touch (check out the photo). Everything else is just acting.

But it's important acting. The key to making this effect work is to *build anticipation*. If you just walk up to someone and flick the match, nobody will be impressed. But if you carefully position the first match in her hand, then make a production of shuffling around to build up static electricity, the anticipation of something dangerous about to happen will put the mark on edge. This tension turns into a yelp when the match rockets up into the air.

DEMONSTRATION

bit.ly/ZG1OMI

If you want to get maximum response, really build up the tension between the match and your fingernail as your approach her. Wait until the matches are about 3 millimeters apart, and when you release your match it'll make a crackling sound as it launches her match right out of her hand.

The Ash

IMPRESSIVENESS:
★★★★☆
CLASS: OPENER/GAG
FACTORS: SUBTLETY!
BE SUBTLE!!

REQUIRES: CIGARETTE,
NEEDLE

I don't smoke. But this trick makes me wish I did.

The Effect: Let an entire cigarette burn without the ash falling.

THE SECRET: **HEY KIDS, REMEMBER: SMOKING IS BAD FOR YOU!**

But for adults who smoke, here's a way to slowly draw all the attention in the room to you. Before you head out to the bar, prepare a couple cigarettes by inserting a long quilting needle into your unlit cigarettes. When you light one of the prepared cigarettes, let the ash sit, and in just a few minutes you'll have an ash 2-3 inches long.

EPISODE

bit.ly/15EYWGb

Remember, *subtlety* is key here: the less you react to this event, the
better it'll look. Just act like you'll get around to tapping the ash
off any minute . . . but keep forgetting. How else can you do essentially
nothing and get everyone to look over your way?

bit.ly/11JmOgj

AUDIO

EQUA✚ION

EPISODE

bit.ly/13smgTL

IMPRESSIVENESS:
★ ★ ★ ★ ☆

CLASS: CLOSER

FACTORS: FRUSTRATINGLY SIMPLE, AGONIZINGLY HARD

REQUIRES: A FISTFULL OF MATCHES OR TOOTHPICKS, OPEN TABLE SPACE

This one's a stumper of a puzzle, yet only uses 4th grade math. It's also another one that I'm going to insist you *actually try* to solve before looking up the answer. With puzzles like these, the quicker you give the answer, the dumber they seem to be. In real life, I'll often leave a puzzle like this to simmer for 20 or 30 minutes before giving up the answer, even if they promise me a beer for it.

The Effect: Using matches (or toothpicks), create the incorrect math equation 1+11+111=1111. Then challenge your friend to move only one match and make the equation true.

AUDIO

bit.ly/14MdBQE

EQUATION   177

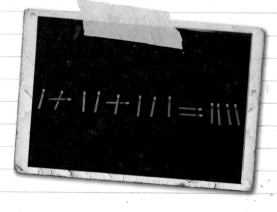

Make sure to point out that the 4 matches on the right side of the equation are correct; it's only the left side that needs fixing. To be even more fair, point out that they can interpret the numbers as roman numerals, hash marks, or traditional Arabic numerals (in truth, all these extra options only serve to make the puzzle even harder).

Oh, and don't let them pull the wise guy move of laying one match across the equals to make a "does not equal" sign!

Once you've spent so much time on this puzzle that you feel like your brain is going to melt, go ahead and read on to discover how simple this puzzle actually is.

THE ANSWER: Take one of the matches from the "11" section, turn it 90 degrees and place it perpendicularly over the middle match in the "111" section.

Properly spaced, the equation then appears as $1 + 1 + 1 + 1 = 1111$!

Out of any puzzle we've covered, this one generates the most emails of alternate solutions. I'm talking about **hundreds** of proposals about everything from laying one match directly on top of another to count them as just one mark to making half-assed, leaning Roman numeral "V's" . . . and none of them as elegant as this solution.

If someone comes up with one of those half-assed solutions and insists it's a good one, just gather some disinterested third parties to act as judges. Once they see the two solutions side-by-side, it's obvious which is the more elegant.

FINAL NOTE: When you set this up, make sure you space out the matches in the "111" section. Your rules clearly state that you can only move *one* match, and you don't want to be accused of violating your own rules in the reveal.

ANSWER VIDEO

bit.ly/ZGnwCJ

HOW TO PREDICT the FUTURE

IMPRESSIVENESS:

★★★★★

CLASS: TWEENER

FACTORS: SMALL PRE-WORK

REQUIRES: DECK OF CARDS, PEN, PAPER

EPISODE

bit.ly/12aH9Tnt

What's better than a card trick? Predicting the *freaking future*, which is exactly what you'll do in this scam.

How It Looks: Your mark shuffles the cards as they like, while you write a simple prediction. Once the cards are shuffled, the mark turns over the cards two-at-a-time, and sorts them in three piles, according to these rules:

- If both cards are red, place them in a "red" pile.
- If both cards are black, place them in a "black" pile.
- If both cards are a mix of one red and one black, toss them into a "discard" pile.

Once the deck is sorted, have them count and tell you the number of cards in the "red" and "black" piles. For example, let's say there are 14 red cards and 10 black ones. Now, show them your prediction, which clearly reads "*THERE WILL BE 4 MORE RED CARDS THAN BLACK*"

The Follow-Up: Even better, you can repeat the effect: Write a new, different prediction. Have the mark repeat all the same steps. This second time, both the red and black piles will be even . . . and that's exactly what your prediction will say: "*BOTH PILES ARE EVEN*".

The Work: First off, you might have trouble believing this, but with a full deck of 52 cards, no matter how much you shuffle them, when you pull off the top 2 cards and separate them into piles as we described, you will *always* end up with two even piles of red and black cards. (If you think about it mathematically, it makes sense. If you don't want to think about it mathematically, just try it a few times and you'll see this is true).

So how do you get 4 more red cards than black ones? By removing 4 black cards and leaving them in the box before you do the trick. Now, no matter what the mark does, if he counts correctly, there will be 4 more red cards in the piles than black cards (which is exactly what your first prediction will say).

The second time you perform this trick, make sure to add in the 4 extra black cards. (The easiest way to do so is to place the cards back into the box as soon as your first performance is finished.) When you pull out all 52 cards, the number of red and black cards will be even. Just make sure your second prediction reads "the piles are even" and you're home free.

AUDIO

bit.ly/XTI5Lk

FACE UP poker

IMPRESSIVENESS:

PART ONE   PART TWO

★★★☆☆   ★★★★★

CLASS: CLOSER

FACTORS: PUNKS A FRIEND, MAKES YOU LOOK CLEVER

REQUIRES: DECK OF CARDS

I love this scam; it's a poker cheat that lets you win twice in a row *and* punks your friend at the same time. It's a totally fair, completely simple contest of "face up draw poker."

The Method: Start off with some smack talk: "You suck at poker." "You got no poker face." "You couldn't win if your life depended on it." . . . and then lay down your real challenge: "You're so terrible, you couldn't beat me in a round of draw poker even if we handpicked our cards from a face up deck." I recommend making your bet totally irresistible. Put up $20 of your money against a single free beer. With a spread that big and a reward so tempting, you'll usually get them to go for it.

When they do, reiterate the rules: the two of you will be playing a completely normal round of draw poker, with the exception that instead of dealing cards out randomly, you'll each get to pick your hands out of the deck. And since you're such a nice guy, you'll even let him go first.

Odds are, he'll go straight for a royal flush. You do the same. Ask him if he wants to discard any cards, or stand pat where he is (he'll likely want to stay put). Once it's clear the round ended in a tie, remind him of the rules of the bet: "even playing with a face up deck, you still couldn't **beat** me . . ." and since you **TIED**, he didn't beat you and owes you a free beer.

This will usually annoy your mark. He'll call shenanigans on your verbal trickery and want to renege on the bet. Offer him an even better solution: "I'll bet you double-or-nothing that if we played again, under the EXACT SAME set of rules, I'd beat you this time!" Hopefully this will pique his interest and rope him into a second round.

Once you begin, off-handedly comment that since he went first last time, you get to go first this time (again, you're just following the regular rules of play). For your first round, pull out all four tens and an ace. This will probably raise an eyebrow, and he'll pull out either a 9-high straight flush or a higher four of a kind (he can't pull out a royal flush, since you've nabbed all the tens). In either case, ask him (just as you did before) if he'd like to discard anything (odds are he will not).

. . . at which point you decide that yes, you would like to discard three of your tens, keeping only the ten and ace of the same suit.

Finally, pull out the jack, queen and king of the same suit, giving you the coveted Royal Flush and **two** free beers.

When we featured this gem on Scam School, I got a **lot** of e-mail from people proposing alternate solutions, claiming the mark could still win. Many of them were asking why the mark couldn't just change his cards for one of your discarded tens. The answer, of course, is that in regular draw poker discards are thrown out in a discard pile and don't come back into the game until the deck is reshuffled.

in the BANK

IMPRESSIVENESS:

★ ★ ☆ ☆ ☆

CLASS: CLOSER

FACTORS: SUPER-SIMPLE, FUN TO WATCH, SOMEWHAT IMPRACTICAL

REQUIRES: BOTTLE, TOOTHPICK OR WOODEN MATCH, DIME

This one's super simple. It's not rocket science, but it's way cool to watch . . .

The Setup: Fold a toothpick in half, making a "V" shape and place it on top of the mouth of a beer bottle. Next, place a dime on top of the folded toothpick and offer the following question:

How do you get the dime into the beer bottle, without touching the bottle, toothpick, or dime, without letting the toothpick fall off the top of the bottle, and without shaking the table?

EPISODE

bit.ly/11JmYt3

AUDIO

bit.ly/11Jn6sz

The Answer: Don't be surprised if your mark just flat-out doesn't believe this one is possible . . . the restrictions are so tight, it seems there's no way to pull it off; however, the solution is unbelievably elegant:

Just drip a couple of drops of water (or any other drink) onto the fold in the toothpick.

The water will cause the wood to expand, opening the toothpick and allowing the dime to drop right in. It may take a long 20–30 seconds for it to happen, but once it does, it's pretty cool: like a ghost hand is pushing it open.

Remember, though: there are a lot of ways people can get lucky and get the dime inside, even without using drops of water. I've seen everything from blowing on the dime, to jumping up and down next to the table . . . even shouting directly into the mouth of the bottle to cause little vibrations. I probably wouldn't risk a beer on this one . . . but *definitely* give it a try.

DEMONSTRATION

bit.ly/ZMw7QO

Stick it with the **FUNNEL** to 'em

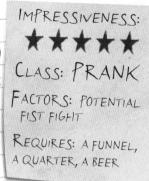

IMPRESSIVENESS:
★ ★ ★ ★ ★

CLASS: PRANK

FACTORS: POTENTIAL FIST FIGHT

REQUIRES: A FUNNEL, A QUARTER, A BEER

Sooner or later when you're pulling scams at the bar, you'll run across someone that's too drunk, annoying, or pushy to pay proper attention. You can usually "stick them to the bar" like we learned a few chapters ago, but someone especially aggressive deserves special treatment . . . which is why we have the atomic bomb of sucker gags: *The Funnel.*

EPSISODE

bit.ly/YKD7hj

The Setup: Start with a demonstration of what the mark's going to try: grab a funnel from behind the bar and tuck it in the waistline of your pants. Balance a quarter on your forehead and slowly tilt your head forward, until the coin falls off and lands in the funnel (if you miss, don't worry: you're only demonstrating the principle, and it's okay if it looks difficult). Explain to the mark that the game is simple: he'll win a free beer from you if he can land the coin from his forehead into the funnel.

Check It!!

AUDIO

bit.ly/13smHgBt

The Execution: Now have the mark mimic your setup: funnel in his pants, head tilted back, quarter on his forehead. Give him a countdown, and just before he starts . . . pour your beer into the funnel, and straight down his pants!

Needless to say, you'll need to choose when to pull this stunt very carefully. And when you do pull it off, be ready for a quick getaway.

This doesn't always have to be done with beer and a funnel at a bar . . . You can quickly improvise a funnel with a rolled up magazine, and you might get less of an angry reaction if you use, say, ice water at a family picnic instead.

the heads/tails con

IMPRESSIVENESS:
★ ★ ★ ★ ☆

CLASS: TWEENER

FACTORS: COMPLICATED LOGIC, PRECISE INSTRUCTION

REQUIRES: COLLECTION OF QUARTERS, AN INTELLIGENT TARGET

EPISODE

bit.ly/15E7Cgi

This one might sound a little heady when you learn it, but trust me: it's *much* easier in practice, and the effect seems impossible. Just do a few trial rounds with a friend before you try it on strangers at the bar.

How It Looks: Start with a fistful of quarters spread out on the table, arranged in a random assortment of "heads" and "tails." You turn around, and ask her to flip over any coin she wants. Then ask her to do it again. And again. Ask if she wants to go again, then ask one more time if she wants to flip another over. It doesn't matter how many times she flips over coins, as long as you know *how many* coins were flipped.

SCAM SCHOOL

Once she's satisfied that there's no way you could know the arrangement or positions of any of the quarters, have her choose any one coin to cover up with her hand.

When you turn back around, just by looking at the exposed quarters, you'll know instantly whether her covered coin is "heads" or "tails."

The Method: Surprisingly enough, it's easy. When you first lay out all the coins, count how many of them are heads-up and remember whether it's an **even** or **odd** number. Make sure you count accurately, because this first count is important.

After you turn around, every time she says she's flipping over a coin, you flip your mental running count from "odd" to "even" or from "even" to "odd." This can get confusing once you're a couple of beers in at the bar, so I recommend using your fingers to keep track under the bar where she can't see. Hold two fingers out for even, one finger for odd, and make sure to change them with each coin flip.

AUDIO

bit.ly/ZlQhpF

Once she says she's done flipping coins, note whether you're currently on EVEN or ODD.

Whatever your final running count is, that's how many heads-up coins are currently on the table.

Read that again: If you're thinking "odd" when she stops, there are now an odd number of heads on the table. If you're on "even" when she stops, then there are an even number of heads.

So when you turn around, count all the heads-up coins you see.

- If the number of heads-up coins you count **matches** your running count: that means she's hiding a **tails**. (In other words, if you expected an even number, and you see an even number, she must not be hiding another heads-up coin)

- If the number of heads-up coins you count **does not match** your running count: then she must be hiding the last **heads-up** coin.

It's SUPER important that you practice your tempo and phrasing during the trick to make sure you absolutely know how many coins are flipped over. If there's any ambiguity, your running count might get off and leave you looking like a chump at the reveal.

the trick that fooled Einstein

Correctly guess how much change is in your friend's pocket!

The Effect: You and your friend pull out some change from your pockets, hold the coins in your hands, and shake 'em. Without looking, and judging from the sound, you're able to accurately describe the *exact difference in value* between your coins and your friend's.

The Method: Not sure if this is true or not, but I learned this trick as "the trick that fooled Einstein." And it's brilliant, thanks to the special phrasing of your prediction.

EPISODE
bit.ly/12aIs4x

To pull this one off, you'll need $2.85 of change in your pocket, comprised of 10 quarters, two dimes, two nickels, and five pennies. Pull out your change, listen to their change shaking, and then confidently announce your three-part prediction: "I have as much change as you do, plus two quarters . . . and enough change left over to bring your total to $2.35."

There's three parts to the prediction:

1. "I have as much change as you do" . . . pull out enough of your change to exactly match your friend's amount.

2. "plus two extra quarters" . . . drop down two quarters.

3. "and enough change left over to bring your total up to $2.35" . . . and sure enough, you'll find that this is exactly true, no matter how much change your friend has.

Why does it work? Because if you look at it algebraically, you're really saying "I have $X + .50 + (\$2.35 - X)$" . . . If you're a math whiz, you know that essentially, you're really saying "I have $2.85," (which is not so impressive). Luckily, the phrase is able to fool just about everyone into thinking you've made an impressive prediction.

This has been one of our all-time most popular Scam School episodes, and I'm kinda shocked at some of the questions I see posted on the YouTube page:

"I'm from the UK/Canada/India/The North Pole . . . how do I do it with [INSERT FOREIGN CURRENCY]???"

Think about it: you do it the exact same way. **Nothing changes just because it's in a different currency**.

"Nice trick, but it won't work if they have more than $2.35 in their pocket!"

First off: that's just about never going to happen. Everybody hates change. But even if they *do* have more than $2.35, I have constructed the following foolproof plan.

- Step 1: Plan on doing the trick exactly as performed in the episode.

- Step 2: As a backup plan, keep five (5) of those new presidential dollars in your left pants pocket.

- Step 3: When pretending to listen to the amount of change they have, ACTUALLY LISTEN TO THE AMOUNT OF CHANGE THEY HAVE.

- Step 4: In the event they sound like they have more money than you, calmly say "Wait a minute," pull out the extra dollars, add them to your cache, cough, then awkwardly mutter "forgot that I had a little more change in there . . . "

- Step 5: Perform the remainder of the effect as depicted in the episode, but making sure to add $5.00 to your final projection.

- Step 6: Prepare yourself for an onslaught of free drinks and offers of sexual intercourse.

NOTE: If the person you're performing for pulls out more than seven dollars and thirty-five cents in change, you are completely and irrevocably screwed. This is your only weakness . . . guard well against this rare and completely lethal counterattack.

Ninja CARD THROWING

EPISODE

bit.ly/13V1U9J

IMPRESSIVENESS: DEPENDS

CLASS: SKILL

FACTORS: PRACTICE, PRACTICE, PRACTICE

REQUIRES: DECK OF CARDS (THE NEWER, THE BETTER)

Hurl playing cards 50 feet at a time. Fling them hard enough to break water balloons, or even embed them into aluminum sheeting.

Sound impossible?

It's not, though it *will* take a lot of practice.

I'm not the world's greatest card thrower, but I'm no slouch, either. Check out one of my luckiest throws from this episode of *Brian Brushwood: On the Road*.

I've learned a few tips to throw cards really far, but first, a **safety warning**:

CHECK OUT BRIAN'S BEST CARD THROW EVER!

bit.ly/A4N6u

At all times be aware that throwing cards can damage any eyes they hit. At all times, make sure that you are taking proper safety precautions and practicing in a suitably safe environment

AUDIO

There's really two different ways to get good distance and power throwing cards . . .

The Hard Way: if you want to become an expert, remember that the key to card throwing is SPIN. The faster the card spins, the more stable its flight, and the farther it will go.

Start by paying attention to your grip: you want to barely clip the very corner of the card between your first and second fingers. The touch should be so light that the card's own momentum should be able to pull it from your grasp.

Next, work on loosening your wrist. The wrist is where you generate all your spin momentum, so it's critical that you get the timing and smooth motion down. To practice, try tossing cards with no arm motion whatsoever . . . only by using the wrist. You'll be surprised to find you can send cards over 20 feet without even using your larger arm muscles.

Once you've got the timing down, then bring in your full arm motion. There are several techniques to the throw, but remember that the arm is where you generate your forward momentum.

Remember that **spin** *is **much more important*** *than forward momentum.*

If you stay focused on that, you'll continue to improve. Just make sure to give yourself a break from time to time . . . it's easy to hurt your arm if you try too hard to fling it all crazy.

"***But Brian!!! This sounds like hard work and practice!!! I want to hurl cards like a badass NOW!!!!***"

I can respect that. Which is why there's always . . .

The Easy Way: If you're having a hard time getting the throw down, just cheat using a rubber band. Spread a rubber band between the thumb and forefinger of your left hand. Now pinch the rubber band onto a playing card about one-third of the way in, pull back, and let fly. The rubber band will give you the exact right mix of spin momentum and forward momentum, and you should be able to get the card sailing over 30 feet.

EASY WAY DEMO

bit.ly/12aIQA5

the one-handed CUT

IMPRESSIVENESS:
★ ★ ★ ☆ ☆

CLASS: FLOURISH

FACTORS: DEXTERITY, PRACTICE

REQUIRES: CARDS, PATIENCE

AUDIO

bit.ly/12FfATp

Sometimes you just want to look like a badass. This one will take some practice, but once you've got it down, it's a neat flourish. More importantly, the skills you build up while practicing this trick will directly improve you card skills for other tricks as well.

EPISODE

bit.ly/ZMwIRS

Performing the One-Handed Cut

The setup is simple: Hold the deck as a block in your left hand, palm-up and pinched between your thumb and four fingers. Start by allowing half the cards to drop as a block from your thumb. When the cards drop, they'll catch at an angle as they rest in the crook of your thumb. This should make it easy to use your index finger to push the dropped block of cards from the other side. Just push and slide it all the way back up against the pad of your thumb, creating a "teepee" or "letter A" shape with the two halves of the deck.

Finally, push your index finger just a little farther upward so that the bottom half of the deck overtakes the top. Once it does, you'll

notice one half of the deck resting on the back of your index finger. At this point, just let gravity do the rest: allow both blocks to drop and the bottom half will now be on top.

Bonus Flourish: If you want to display the bottom card of the deck with a little flourish, follow these steps. Perform the one-handed cut exactly as you've learned it, but at the very end, prevent the two halves from falling all the way on to each other by inserting your middle finger between them. The top half will balance on your middle finger, and while it rests there, if you extend your middle finger it will drag out the bottom card of the pack.

Once that card is out, keep rolling your middle finger around the side of the deck, pulling the card with it until it ends up displayed face-up over the face-down deck of cards.

DEMONSTRATION

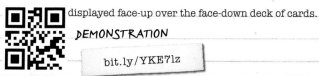

bit.ly/YKE7lz

SIX MATCHES

6 4△

FOUR TRIANGLES

IMPRESSIVENESS:
★ ★ ★ ☆ ☆

CLASS: CLOSER

FACTORS: CHALLENGING PUZZLE

REQUIRES: STRANGELY ENOUGH ... 6 WOODEN MATCHES

Here's another tough match puzzle *almost* guaranteed to win you a drink. Remember, it's the tricks that get you attention, but selling the answers to puzzles gets you the drinks.

The Rules: Using 6 matchsticks or toothpicks, create 4 equilateral triangles. All 4 triangles have to be the same size, and the sides of each triangle have to be exactly one matchstick long.

It sounds impossible, and 99% of the time the mark will just give up. Grab some matches and try to work this one out.

If you've attempted this puzzle for 25 days, lost your job, wife, and home, you've earned a peek at the answer.

bit.ly/17UIZeG

EPISODE

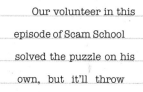

Our volunteer in this episode of Scam School solved the puzzle on his own, but it'll throw most people into a fit of frustration.

Unlike other match puzzles covered on the show, the solution to this one adds a third dimension, forcing your mark to think a bit outside the box before coming up with anything close to the right answer.

Create the 3D solution by laying the bottom triangle down flat and holding the 3 remaining matches above to create a tetrahedron. This works best by pinching the matches' ends together and allowing the opposite ends to spread out individually toward each of the bottom triangle's corners. In the diagram shown, you can see how the 4 triangles are represented in the 3D shape. The answer won't be able to stand up on its own, but that won't stop you from earning your free drink.

AUDIO

bit.ly/12aJb61

Epic POWERBAND Scam

EPISODE

bit.ly/dYhqfl

IMPRESSIVENESS:
★ ★ ★ ★ ☆

CLASS: TWEENER, LESSON

FACTORS: FEELS LIKE MAGIC FOR THEM, IMPORTANT LESSON

REQUIRES: RANDOM "MAGIC" OBJECT

I think this may be one of the episodes of Scam School I'm most proud of. Most of the stuff we teach on the show is good to score you a free beer or maybe get the girl's number, but this episode was different: There are people out there selling magic bracelets that they *know for a fact* have absolutely no evidence that they actually work . . . And it was awesome to expose some the exact techniques they use to create their convincing demonstrations.

The Scam: Sell a 3-dollar rubber wristband for $30, $40, or even $50, by convincing people of its amazing properties.

You've seen those bracelets out there, right? The ones that are supposed to use holograms to align your energy and give you better balance? I can't comment on whether those work (you know, the whole "you can't prove a negative" thing), but I know for a fact that *our* power bands don't work.

AUDIO

bit.ly/ZMx0bm

Thanks to the Skeptic Bros of Australia, we hit the bars armed with a fistful of "placebo bands." These beauties look just like those famous ones, but are 100% guaranteed to *not* have any magic holograms in them.

Oh, and surprise: they can be shown to work just as well as the "real" thing.

The key is to learn a few physical tests that use leverage and psychology to convince people that they're getting stronger or more balanced. Once you have these mastered, you can convince anyone that *anything* is a magic charm that will improve their balance.

Lateral Balance Test: Have them stand up straight, with their arms fully extended each direction, and balance on one foot.

Without the band, place just two fingers on the elbow of the arm opposite the foot they're standing on. Push down with only the slightest constant pressure, and you'll pull them off balance easily.

Wearing the band, have them stand in exactly the same posture, but this time, as you push on their arm, aim your pressure directly at the foot they're balancing upon. This will feel to them as if you're doing the exact same moves, but they'll be

surprised that they have considerably more balance.

Drive home the strength of their newfound balance by increasing the pressure on their elbow. Use first one, then two hands and lean in with all your strength . . . they'll be able to handle it, because it's not the *strength* of pressure that matters, it's the *direction*. But subjectively, all they'll be able to notice is *how much harder* you're pushing on them. They'll be convinced they now possess greater balance.

Pitch Balance Test: For this one, have your sucker stand up straight and interlace their fingers in a cup shape behind their back. Place your fist into the cup of her hands, and gently push down, aiming for the spot just an inch or so behind their heels.

It should take very little effort to pull your volunteer off balance, tipping her backward. This is a more powerful demonstration as it's awkward and uncomfortable for the volunteer at the moment they lose balance.

Give her the band to wear, and this time as you press down, aim

for the spot right in *front* of her heels. This very minor adjustment makes a **big** difference. Just like before, she'll feel nothing different in your motions, but have the sensation of *much* better balance.

The Twist: Have your volunteer stand up straight, feet shoulder-width apart. Have him extend his right arm with his index finger pointed. Tell him "Okay, now turn your body to your left, until you can't go any more." When he stops turning, take a moment to note what he's currently pointing at. That will set your "baseline" measure.

After putting the band back on, explain carefully that something amazing is going to happen: "Now that the band is in place, you're going to be able to turn at least 20% farther. Try it."

He'll be astonished at how much farther he can twist while wearing the band.

The phrasing of this is important: the first time, there's no mention of making this a contest, or even explanation of what you're up to. They're just told to turn left until they can't. But the *second* time, you've made them a challenge and set a goal of "20%" farther. Now that (1) they know what to expect, and (2) have a contest in mind, they'll shock themselves by how much farther they can turn.

Remember: There are several variations on all of these tests, but they all rely on similar principles. You'll see variations of these tests at everything from motivational seminars to quack medicine practitioners.

2 CARD PREDICTION

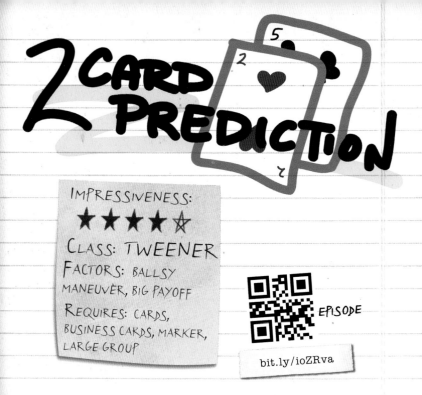

IMPRESSIVENESS:
★ ★ ★ ★ ☆

CLASS: TWEENER

FACTORS: BALLSY MANEUVER, BIG PAYOFF

REQUIRES: CARDS, BUSINESS CARDS, MARKER, LARGE GROUP

EPISODE

bit.ly/ioZRva

This one's so quick, simple, and easy that you'll be tempted to think it won't fool anyone. Trust me: every time I've pulled this one, it's gotten a strong reaction. The method is so simple you can do it right in front of them without anyone having so much as a clue.

The Trick: Have a deck of cards thoroughly shuffled. Grab the deck, and as you double-check to see if they want to shuffle any more, secretly glimpse the top and bottom cards in the deck as shown.

bit.ly/XTJG3y

AUDIO

Then pull out a business card to make your secret prediction. Jot down your prediction (which will be the two cards you just glimpsed on the top and bottom of the deck), then hand the business card (prediction-side-down) to another volunteer and ask her to slide the card in anywhere she wants in the deck.

To be even *more* fair, turn to yet another volunteer and ask if she wants to move it somewhere else. They can take as many times as they want to keep moving the business card. Once they're satisfied, spread the cards and separate the deck right where the business card sits.

Square up each half of the deck in each of your hands, and make sure to keep the prediction card prediction-side down on top of the packet in your left hand. To prove that you really did make a prediction, turn to just one person and show her what you wrote. But here's the important part: turn over the prediction by *rolling the business card over* from the top of your left hand pack onto the top of your right hand packet.

Once she's seen it, flip the prediction back over, but *leave it on the right-hand packet*. As you recap how fair everything's been, drop the packet from your left hand onto the right-hand packet. What you've done is actually *move* the prediction from wherever they originally put it to the spot right between the top and bottom cards. It's now sitting *right between the two cards that match the prediction!*

This is such a bold maneuver, you might be certain people will catch it. Trust me: as long as your moves are natural, and as long as you keep the conversation afloat, nobody will notice.

After a few seconds of time delay, you can spread the deck, remove the prediction and the cards above and below it . . . then show that all three match!

bit.ly/15E8AJk

DEMONSTRATION

π Pi Day MAGIC

IMPRESSIVENESS:

★ ★ ★ ★ ★

CLASS: TWEENER

FACTORS: MATH, PRESENTATION

REQUIRES: CALCULATOR

James Grime is a freakin' wizard. He's the mathematician from Cambridge University who calculated the true odds in the "Playing the Odds" chapter (page 127), and a couple of years ago he came to me with an idea to celebrate Pi Day by performing the biggest interactive magic trick I'd ever seen. Pi Day (March 14th, or 3/14 — get it?) is an all-around geeky "holiday" popular on the internet, and it seemed like the perfect event to attempt a math-related, internet-based magic trick.

With the help of some programmer friends, James developed a script that controlled our twitter accounts and allowed us to perform the trick individually for thousands of people worldwide, all day long. It was a total blast, and the trick is a real fooler. James mentioned that he's been able to fool countless math professors with it, and it only requires a calculator. You can perform it in person, over the phone, or (as we did) even over twitter.

AUDIO

bit.ly/11yOr3c

The Setup:

Have your friend grab a calculator and start multiplying random single digits together. Have him multiply as many digits as he wants, the more random the numbers, the better. Make a string something like 6 x 2 x 3 x 7 x 4 x 8 x 2 x 9 x 3 . . . and so on. Have him stop once he's made a 7-, 8-, or 9-digit number somewhere between one million and one billion.

From this gigantic number, have him choose any single digit to be his "secret" number. That's the one you're going to try to figure out. Amazingly, even though you had no idea what numbers he multiplied and no idea what his final gigantic number was . . . all you need to hear are all the digits except his secret number, and you'll be able to guess it correctly.

The Math: This sounds absolutely impossible, and when James performed it on me I was completely stunned. The key to this trick is to emphasize the *randomness* of the single digits they choose multiply. The trick won't work if somebody just keeps multiplying 7's repeatedly, so make sure to specifically mention that they need to use a lot of *different* numbers when they multiply.

The odds are, as they keep multiplying random numbers, sooner or later they'll hit a multiple of 9. Once they do, no matter what they choose to multiply afterward, the result will also be a multiple of 9.

And there are some tricky things you can do with multiples of 9.

One property of multiples of 9 is that all of the digits that make up the number will always add up to be a multiple of 9. Look at a few examples:

- 9 x 8 = 72, and 7 + 2 = 9

- 9 x 4 = 36, and 3 + 6 = 9

- 9 x 11 = 99, and 9 + 9 = 18 (which is also a multiple of 9)

It even works with really, really big multiples of 9:

- 9 x 4 x 7 x 2 x 6 x 5 x 2 x 8 x 7 = 1,693,440, and 1 + 6 + 9 + 3 + 4 + 4 + 0 = 27 (another multiple of 9)

So if you're given all the numbers *except* their secret number, you can figure out their secret number by adding up all the other digits and calculating how much more you'd need to add to reach a multiple of 9.

Let's take the number we created above, 1,693,440. If your mark selected "6" as his secret number, he'd tell you all the other digits, and you'd add up 1 + 9 + 3 + 4 + 4 + 0 to get 21. The next-highest multiple of 9 is 27, so you'd subtract 21 from 27 to get his secret number: 6.

Another example, just for practice: I've got a secret number, but all the other digits are 4, 3, 4, 5, 6, and 0. If you add them together, 4 + 3 + 4 + 5 + 6 + 0 = 22. 27 is the next highest multiple of 9, so 27 − 22 = 5, my secret number.

"But what if they don't hit 9 when they're multiplying random numbers?"

Incredibly, the trick will probably *still* work! They might miss 9, but as long they hit 3 twice, you'll still be in multiples of 9. Just make sure to emphasize that they use as many different numbers as they can to make their number as unpredictable as possible.

example

2, 641, 889, 250
secret number

2, 641, 8_9, 250
add all digits except
secret number

$2 + 6 + 4 + 1 + 8 + 9 + 2 + 5 = 37$

count up to next multiple of 9
then subtract previous total

$45 - 37 = 8$

Secret number!

One Special Case: The only time the trick hits a snag is when you add up all the digits and discover the sum is *already* a multiple of 9. When this happens, it means their secret digit is either a 0 or 9. I'll usually handle this by saying "Hmm ... this is a tough one ... it's definitely a 0 or a 9 ..." As I say this, I'll pay careful attention to their expression. Often times, they'll react right as I say their number. If they don't give any reaction, I'll make an educated guess based on the other digits. If the digits are 2 7 0 0 0 0 0, then I'll guess their secret number is also a 0. If the digits are 3 9 1 1 0 4 0, then I'll be more likely to guess 9.

~~BONDAGE~~

(for fun and profit)

Like tying people up and watching them squirm? This scam is for you.

The Scam: Get two marks. Tie the first one's wrists together manacle-style with a rope (or their own necktie). Tie their wrists loosely "for their comfort," but tell them they can't take the rope off their wrists. Tie the second mark's wrists together, linking his rope with the first sucker's.

Challenge them to unlink themselves *without untying the ropes.*

EPISODE

bit.ly/gJ4SFC

bit.ly/15E8Rfn

AUDIO

With any luck, your marks will try all sorts of Twister-style moves to get themselves unhitched. With a little more luck, a large crowd will gather and laugh at their tomfoolery.

Eventually, most people at some point actually end up climbing through each other's arms ... it's awesome, and does nothing to help them out.

The Solution: Their problem is that they're thinking linearly. They're essentially two links in a chain, and no amount of big twisting will get them out.

The real solution is simple, yet devious. Remember how you tied their wrists loosely? All they have to do is thread the rope through the wrist hole, wrap it over one hand, pull it back through and ... *poof*! Freedom!

MIND BLOWING PHONE CALCULATOR TRICK

IMPRESSIVENESS:

★ ★ ★ ★ ★

CLASS: TWEENER

FACTORS: BORROWED PHONE, CAN BE IMPROMPTU OR PRE-SET

REQUIRES: IPHONE OR ANDROID PHONE

bit.ly/eDCuAi

EPISODE

I absolutely *love* this trick. It's totally brilliant, completely impromptu, and devilishly clever . . . so of course I had nothing to do with its creation.

How It Looks: First you write down a prediction. Then ask everyone around you for a string of numbers: birth dates, addresses, dress sizes, anything numeric. All of these numbers are multiplied together using a borrowed phone calculator (you don't even need to be the one holding the calculator!). Finally, someone presses "equals," and the final number is displayed. The final number *exactly* matches your prediction, you are instantly hailed as a national hero, and you go on to an exciting career in politics. *Probably.*

How it's Done: This is all based on the fact that while the iPhone calculator *looks* like a simple "dumb calculator," it's actually a powerful, fully-functional scientific calculator. The difference is that simple calculators only perform one function at a time, and they're performed in the exact order that you type them in. Scientific calculators, however, will follow the proper math order of operations, in which multiplications are always performed before additions.

Here's how you take advantage of this: before you start the trick, type in whatever number you want to force, plus zero, then hit the times button. Now, no matter what numbers are added to the equation, the expression is:

(your number) + 0 x (any number) x (any number) x (any number) . . .

Since the calculator follows proper order of operations, the first thing it will do is handle the multiplications, and since anything times 0 is 0, the expression becomes:

(your number) + 0 = (your number)

AUDIO

bit.ly/ZlSiC8

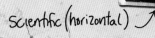

normal (vertical orientation)

DEMONSTRATION

Scientific (horizontal) ↗

If you want to use your own phone for this, just pre-set the first part of the expression and switch to another app. The iPhone will remember what you had already entered. If you want to borrow an iPhone, you should be able to sneakily enter the first part before announcing that you want to try a trick.

In either case, keep in mind that when you begin, the "x" key will be highlighted (since it's the last one you pressed). To cover this, I make sure to keep the phone in my hand until I start to enter the first digits given. As soon as I start entering numbers, I stop and announce "Oh, crap! I shouldn't even touch the phone . . . you guys might think I'm doing something sneaky. Here, you hold it and enter all the numbers in." The sooner you can get the phone into someone else's hand, the better.

If you want to be *really* sneaky, you could borrow someone's phone earlier in the day and pre-set the number. It'll sit there like a trap, waiting all day for you to trigger the brain explosion . . .

Petals around the Rose

bit.ly/17fZ3Gw

EPISODE

IMPRESSIVENESS:
★ ★ ★ ★ ☆

CLASS: PUZZLE

FACTORS: HILARIOUSLY, AGONIZINGLY FRUSTRATING

REQUIRES: 5 DICE

Legend has it that Bill Gates saw this puzzle at a party, and it utterly stumped and confounded him. Other folks at the same party figured it out almost instantly, but Gates' logical, analytic mind just couldn't crack it. This one works best with a group of people, and be warned: it will probably occupy the next 40 minutes or more.

bit.ly/11yOPPmt

AUDIO

The Game: Grab 5 dice and the attention of your friends. Let them know that you're a member of a secret, ancient order, known as the "Potentate of the Rose," and that they can join only if they solve your game:

"The name of the game is 'Petals Around the Rose', and the name is important. That's the first thing I can tell you. I can also tell

you that the answer will always be an even number, and I can tell you the answer for any throw of the dice."

At this point, roll the 5 dice:

"For example, for this roll, the answer is 6."

PETALS AROUND THE ROSE

Roll the dice again:

"... and in this roll, the answer is zero. If you can solve the puzzle, then you become a member of the Potentate of the Rose, and are sworn to keep the secret."

Roll again:

"The answer is 10."

Now at this point, you'll almost certainly start getting questions, asking "what if . . . ?" "can I . . . ?" or "is it such and such?" *This is the important part*: You **must** respond to these questions only with the following:

I can only tell you three things: The name of the game is 'Petals Around the Rose,' and the name is important. I can also tell you that the answer will always be an even number or zero. Finally, I can tell you the results of any throw of the dice.

It's the repetition of this actual phrase that is going to utterly frustrate them. They're going to have to rely completely on their wits if they want to join the order, no compromises.

Which brings me to my challenge to you: do **you** want to honestly join the Potentate of the Rose, or are you going to be a faker, a liar, and a heretic? If you want to join honestly, I've given you a couple of rolls to work with. If you can figure out the simple system to get the correct answers for these rolls, you're in. If not, you're a faker, a liar, and a cheat . . . like me. And if that's you then you can find your answer on the next page

Answer Key

The Answer: Remember the first clue ... "The name of the game is 'Petals Around the Rose,' and the name is important."

Now look at the dice, and think of them not as numbers, but a simple visual representation of a rose.

The dot in the center is the rose. The dots surrounding it are the petals. In this case, the 5 has a rose and 4 petals around it, and the 3 has a rose with 2 petals. A 1 would have a rose but no petals, and all the even numbered dice would have petals, but no rose.

To know the answer, for each throw you simply count up the number of petals around the roses.

Now go forth and frustrate all your friends!

$2x(8^3)^4 = 10$ $\frac{23}{4} \times \frac{5}{2.1} = y^{2+4}$

(fake) CRAZY MATH SKILLS

$42 \div 4.113$ $\sqrt{2.7}$

IMPRESSIVENESS: ★★★☆☆

CLASS: TWEENER

FACTORS: RACE, FAKE TALENT, A LOT OF PROCESS

REQUIRES: STUFF TO WRITE WITH

The Effect: Without letting you see his work, a friend jots down a long column of 10 numbers. The numbers start in the single digits, but go well into the triple digits. The paper is turned over, and your friend is given a calculator. The challenge is simple: once you flip back over the paper so both of you can see the numbers, the race begins to add them all together. He gets to use his calculator, but you have to add them all up in your mind.

Incredibly, when the race starts, you'll shout out the correct answer *in less than 5 seconds* **and** without any help from a calculator.

EPISODE

bit.ly/195zDa

The Secret: The random column of numbers is generated
in a specific way. Tell him to start the column with *any two* **single-
digit numbers**. Generate a third number by adding the first and
second numbers together. Add the second and third number to create
a fourth; add the third and fourth to create a fifth, and so on until
you have your column of ten numbers.

Creating all the numbers this way will create a Fibonacci-like
sequence of numbers, which will have special properties. Even though
the first two single-digit numbers are truly random, and nobody
could have predicted in advance what numbers will make up the
column, you'll be able to use one of these properties as a shortcut
to get the total instantly.

As soon as the race begins, look for the seventh number down.
Multiply that number times 11, and you'll have the total for the entire
column.

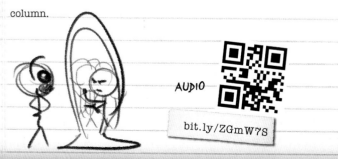

AUDIO

bit.ly/ZGmW7S

example

Fast   **Slow**

(41 × 11)

5
2
7
9
16
25
(41)
66
107
+ 173
‾‾‾‾‾
451

seventh number

4 _ 1
(add)
↓
451

No matter what the first two starting numbers are, the seventh one down will always be a two-digit number, so you'll need to learn a trick to quickly multiply it by 11 in your mind.

How to multiply 2-digit numbers times 11:

● Step 1: in your mind, split apart the first and second digit and create a blank spot in-between.

● Step 2: fill the blank spot with the first and second digit added together.

● Step 3: if the first and second digit add up to be a single digit number, you're done. That 3 digit number is the total of the entire column.

● Step 3a: if the first and second digit add up to be a two-digit number, move the tens digit over to the first digit of your grand total, and just keep the second digit where it is.

A huge thanks goes to magician Curt Anderson for showing me this classic! Check out more of Curt at Magicurt.com.

the BLOW HARD Scam

This one's a classic! They look like an idiot, and you prove that you're smarter than they are. What's not to love?

The Setup: Fold a bottle cap in half and place it inside the lip of a bottle set on its side, balanced right on the edge. Tell your friends that all they have to do to win a free drink is blow the bottle cap into the bottle.

Sounds simple, right? However, once they start, every puff of air only blows the bottle cap *out* of the bottle. It's a really surprising effect, and most people immediately want to know why it won't work.

EPISODE
bit.ly/15F4iRK

bit.ly/10b951N

AUDIO

The answer is in the air pressure. When they blow into the bottle, air pressure is increased on the inside, forcing the bottle cap out.

The Reversal: However you *still* can succeed where they fail: grab a small cocktail straw (the smaller, the better), and use short, sharp blasts of air, blown very close to the bottle cap. By using such a precisely-targeted blast of air, you'll be able to carefully blow the bottle cap all the way inside the bottle.

bit.ly/12FgX12

DEMONSTRATION

THE INDESTRUCTIBLE dollar

IMPRESSIVENESS:
★★★★☆
CLASS: TWEENER
FACTORS: PRE-SET REQUIRED, NEED SPECIAL PROPS
REQUIRES: DOLLAR BILL, PEN, PLAYING OR BUSINESS CARD

Some of my favorite episodes of Scam School were those featuring Rich "The Ice Breaker" Ferguson. I particularly loved this trick—it felt like nothing less than real magic to me, and I couldn't believe that a trick this good could be so easy to perform.

How It Looks: Grab a business card, playing card, or coaster and fold it in half. Inside, place a folded bill from your wallet, pulling the outer flap down to provide a more exposed view. Finally, place a pen, knife, or any other stabby implement in the center of the bill. Have your friend stab the pen down, all the way through the bill and card. He'll actually *feel* the penetration as the card and bill are torn. When the pen is removed, you can actually see through the hole left behind. There's absolutely no question that the bill has been punctured . . . which is what makes it so amazing when the bill is removed from the card and shown to be completely whole.

EPISODE

bit.ly/qfFkEu

DEMONSTRATION
(WORTH WATCHING!)

bit.ly/12aMxpp

How It's Done: This one requires a small amount of preparation beforehand. Before the trick, cut or tear a small "half-moon" flap along the bill's seal. The seal will provide excellent camouflage to cover the flap, and if you pinch the bill over the seal, there's no chance anyone will notice anything odd. When placing the bill in the card, make sure the seal and trap door is just below the edge of the card, and pull the other flap down just before the seal.

When you place the pen in the bill, simply run it through the trap door and slide it down along the outside of the bill to the bottom of the card. For emphasis, you can pinch the card on all sides to clearly show the shape of the pen running down the center of the bill. When your friend pushes the pen through, he'll definitely feel the penetration of the card, and assume it's penetrating the bill as well.

flap closed

flap open →

bit.ly/XTKDcd

When you remove the bill, reach in and pinch right on the seal as you pull it out. This will cover the trap-door, but more importantly reset the position of it so the bill can be loosely handled. As soon as the bill comes out, all the focus will be on the center of the bill. As long as you cover your secret trap-door, everyone can look as closely as they want: there's nothing to find.

Two thoughts on this trick: First, don't let the fact that this trick requires preparation keep you from trying it. It's going to get a big response, and in a busy, talkative group you can probably tear out the trap door right under the table without anyone noticing.

Second, remember that once the bill is removed, you're going to have to perform a delicate dance: you've gotta keep them from seeing that trap-door, but at all times handle the bill as if you're not the least bit concerned about it. The more you perform this trick, the easier this will become. Pay attention to your body language: your posture, your eyes, the looseness of your grip on the bill.

Major thanks to Rich Ferguson for coming on the show and teaching this one to us . . . in real life performance, it feels like nothing less than magic!

All of these combine to nonverbally tell your mark whether there's anything fishy going on.

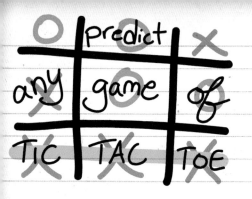

IMPRESSIVENESS:
★ ★ ★ ★ ★
CLASS: TWEENER
FACTORS: IMPOSSIBLE PREDICTION
REQUIRES: STUFF TO WRITE WITH

The Effect: Just for grins, you play a casual game of tic-tac-toe with a friend. All of the moves are totally fair, and they truly have a free choice of where to play every single move of the game.

Yet once you end in a tie game (as almost every game of tic-tac-toe does), you flip over your prediction of how the match would end up . . . and the prediction matches the game perfectly.

How it's Done: First time I had this one performed on me, I was utterly and completely fooled. This is an absolutely brilliant effect from the genius Martin Gardner that you can do anytime, anywhere.

bit.ly/cpQULV

EPISODE

bit.ly/1Ob9g0y

AUDIO

To set up the trick, quietly write down this exact endgame of tic-tac-toe (pictured below), and place it face down nearby. As long as you're subtle, you can probably do this right in front of your target. Don't make a big deal about labeling it as your "prediction" and don't announce that you're about to do a trick.

To get maximum impact on this, it should feel like a totally organic experience.

To remember this specific endgame pattern, in my mind I always think of the name of this effect as "Oxo, Oxx, Xox," as if I was reading the three lines as words. Remembering this name phonetically makes memorizing the pattern a cinch.

Start playing a game of tic-tac-toe by drawing the board and placing an x in the middle. As you play, simply follow two rules:

1. If they place an O in a **corner** box, place your X in the box **clockwise** from it.

2. If they place an O in a **side** box, place your X in the box **counter-clockwise** from it.

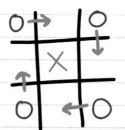

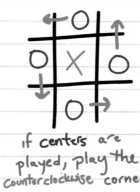

if corners are played, play the clockwise center

if centers are played, play the counterclockwise corner

No matter how they play, as long as you follow these rules, you will end up with a draw that will exactly match your prediction. Seriously . . . try it for yourself a few times.

Two important notes on this effect:

First, the player actually needs to play to win for this to work. Obviously, if he let you get three X's in a row, it won't match the prediction. To fix this, I'll introduce the game by drawing the board and placing my X, then mention "Hey— let's play tic-tac-toe. If you win I'll buy you a drink." Now he's got motivation both to play and try to win, and has no idea he's actually participating in the setup to a prediction effect.

Second, although the game will always match the prediction, it may not match the same orientation. Before you turn over your prediction, note whether your game exactly matches your "Oxo, Oxx, Xox" orientation. If it doesn't, figure out which way you'll need to turn your prediction to have it match when you flip it over.

the end

You made it to the end of *Scam School*, but don't worry, there's much more to come. In the meantime, why not check out our show at ScamSchool.tv where you can see hundreds of full episodes. If you want to hear more about *Scam School*, we'll keep you up-to-date with the latest information over at scamschoolbook.com. (Oh, and make sure to sign up on the email list for future updates.)

Our plan is to create two more volumes in the next year, each as rich and detailed as the one you just read. I'm certain you have valuable feedback on this book (and what you'd like to see in upcoming volumes), so please feel free to write me at brian@shwood.com

The important thing is that you now have 70 fun, impressive tricks to choose from. So my homework assignment to you is to pick any 5 tricks, practice them, and become really good at them before trying to master them all.

For more information on Brian, visit shwood.com Or visit the BBpedia.net, the fan-made, all-things-Brian wiki.

I mean this: people ask me all the time what trick they should do in situation x, y, or z . . . And the truth is, why you really need to do is discover you own character. These effects are meant only as social lubricant to allow your natural personality to come through.

The more you perform and interact with other people, the more of your own personality you'll discover.

As I tell most beginners: whatever's wrong with your performance, it's nothing that 1000 shows won't fix.

So get out there and fail. A lot. Build up an epic arsenal of failure stories, and share them with me and your friends. By the time you're through, you'll find yourself much more skilled, prepared, and (most importantly) much more interesting.

—Brian

To keep up with Brian's adventures across the nation, on the Internet, and elsewhere, follow him on your favorite social network.

And, get updates about the latest Brian projects by signing up for the Brian Brushwood mailing list at shwood.com/social

facebook.com/shwood   google.com/+shwood

twitter.com/@shwood

FEEL FREE TO USE THESE PAGES TO
CONCOCT YOUR OWN SOCIAL MAGIC!

WRITE DOWN NOTES TO IMPROVE HOW
YOU PERFORM!

AND EVEN IMPROVE UPON THE SCAMS,
TRICKS, AND TOOLS I'VE GIVEN YOU SO
FAR!

CELLAR DOOR